9/05 - 4

X3

1/05

Feng Shui
Your Work Spaces

Feng Shui
Your Work Spaces

Sharon Stasney

Sterling Publishing Co., Inc. New York

A Sterling/Chapelle Book

Chapelle, Ltd.

- Jo Packham
- Sara Toliver
- Cindy Stoeckl

- Editor: Lana Hall
- Photography: Kevin Dilley for Hazen Photography
  Sharon Stasney
- Photo Stylist: Suzy Skadburg
- Art Director: Karla Haberstich
- Copy Editor: Marilyn Goff
- Graphic Illustrator: Kim Taylor
- Staff: Kelly Ashkettle, Areta Bingham, Donna Chambers, Emily Frandsen, Mackenzie Johnson, Susan Jorgensen, Jennifer Luman, Melissa Maynard, Barbara Milburn, Lecia Monsen, Desirée Wybrow

Library of Congress Cataloging-in-Publication Data

Stasney, Sharon
    Feng shui your work spaces / Sharon Stasney.
        p. cm.
    "A Sterling/Chapelle book."
    Includes index.
    ISBN 1-4027-0402-X
    1. Feng shui. I. Title
BF1779.F4 S796 2004
133.3'337--dc22
                            2003019007

10 9 8 7 6 5 4 3 2 1

Published by Sterling Publishing Co., Inc.
387 Park Avenue South, New York, NY 10016
©2004 by Sharon Stasney
Distributed in Canada by Sterling Publishing
c/o Canadian Manda Group, One Atlantic Avenue, Suite 105
Toronto, Ontario, Canada M6K3E7
Distributed in Great Britain by Chrysalis Books
64 Brewery Road, London N79NT, England
Distributed in Australia by Capricorn Link (Australia) Pty. Ltd.
P.O. Box 704, Windsor, NSW 2756, Australia
Printed in China
All Rights Reserved

Sterling ISBN 1-4027-0402-X

Write Us

If you have any questions or comments, please contact:

Chapelle Ltd., Inc.
P.O. Box 9252, Ogden, UT 84409
(801) 621-2777 • (801) 621-2788 Fax
e-mail: chapelle@chapelleltd.com
web site: chapelleltd.com

Introduction

Make the energy of your environment a conscious part of your life.

—author

What you do for your "life's work" is not simply how you earn money in the world, it is how you respond to and fulfill your life's calling. The word "vocation" literally means "a calling."

To be fully satisfying and meaningful, your life's work must:

- bring you into contact with that deeper part of yourself that holds your secrets and your wisdom;

- take you beyond yourself and provide a place for you in the structure of humanity;

- integrate the multiple facets of your personality (your many gifts, skills, and experiences) and provide a full expression of those integrated facets;

- allow you to interact with the natural environment in a mutually supportive and beneficial way.

Feng Shui Your Work Spaces examines your office environment with these needs in mind. Whether you work in an office, a storefront, or a manufacturing plant, feng shui focuses your awareness on how the arrangement of your space defines and affects your

5

One way or another, we all have to find what best fosters the flowering of our humanity in this contemporary life, and dedicate ourselves to that.

—Joseph Campbell

personal development, as well as your work. In fact, this Chinese art views work as a vehicle for further defining and expressing the self. The shape and size of your desk, the comfort factor of your chair, and the colors on your walls all influence your mental and emotional states of being. By carefully selecting decor and placements that support your desired result, your office becomes a physical manifestation of your life's direction. To design your space with conscious intent and deep caring is to position yourself for a rich and meaningful life.

Table of Contents

Setting up shop

The choices you make when setting up your office establish energy patterns that will affect your body and your work for as long as you remain in the space. This chapter will help you select and place key furniture pieces to establish energy patterns that both reflect and support you.

Fabric panels on rollers provide privacy and personal space when needed and can be moved when the space is used for team functions. Incorporating flexible walls into your office design will allow you to shift the function of each space as often as needed, without incurring the expense of building or tearing down cubicles.

Your office has good feng shui if it:

- reflects your personality;

- supports your physical body;

- creates mental and physical states that encourage you to do your best work;

- provides physical, emotional, and interpersonal safety;

- balances risk-taking, relaxation, and focused concentration;

- supports your financial goals;

- keeps you grounded in the present while opening future possibilities.

Horizontal surfaces function as fertile ground, allowing potential ideas and projects to be manifested into reality. This expansive work surface represents a tremendous capacity for productivity. Note the creative use of storage units that keep items off the desk's surface, yet handy.

Selecting the right desk

Your desk represents manifestation on a physical plane. This horizontal surface allows you to bring forth what lies hidden within, birthing what the Chinese called *"spirit chi"* (potential energy) in a physical form. This is the role of all horizontal surfaces, but it is especially crucial for desks. Selecting the right desk will enable you to bring forth your best inner creations into the world.

The desk area and the items on your desk form your "immediate work environment." Use this area to balance out what is happening in your larger work environment. For example, if you have a sharp, sarcastic manager, you can balance that person's sharpness by selecting a wooden desk and using soft cream and brown colors.

Materials

Wood. In general, wood is solid, sturdy, long lasting, and reliable. By selecting a wooden desk, you express your desire for reliability, predictability, and support in your work. Various woods have cultural and social implications, which are important in determining how your choice will mesh with your ideal client's perception.

When selecting the materials for your desk, ask yourself:

- Does this choice create a positive impression for my ideal client?

- Does it represent a lifestyle with which they want to associate themselves?

- Maple. The modern elegance of the 1990s, maple is still a favorite. The turn of the millennium saw an increase of maple mixed with black or chrome, bringing maple office furniture into the 2000s. Maple is sleek, sophisticated, and current. However, its very sleekness could make it appear untrustworthy if your ideal customer prefers things that are "tried-and-true."

The light finish and smooth surface of maple creates a yang mental effect. Maple furniture keeps your energy in your head, increasing your ability to focus, rather than allowing it to sink down into the emotional body. If coworkers or clients tend to dump their emotions and moods on you, consider a maple desk.

- Oak. Sturdy and solid, oak represents longevity. This very longevity can be a detriment, however, since the oak desk of fifty years ago is still around today. Oak office furniture was a trend in the 1970s, became available to ordinary households and offices in the 1980s, and went out of trend in the 1990s. Depending on your business market, oak might mark you as being behind the times, out of touch with current trends.

- Teak. A relatively inexpensive wood, teak brings the exotic flavor of Indonesia and Java to the office. Originally, it was primarily used for shipbuilding; and teak still holds the mystery of adventures and faraway lands, making it a welcome addition to many contemporary office spaces. If you select teak wood for your office, make certain it is treated, as it is known for cracking and splitting in drier climates. Many office-furniture lines now carry a teak look-alike that brings the warm mid-toned color into the space without the cracking problems of the original wood.

- Pine. Often painted, pine has been versatile enough to escape serious trending. Moving beyond its country origins, pine furniture is currently available in numerous forms and styles, with straight or curved legs, rustic or smooth surfaces. Still, pine is easily available and connotes familiarity and comfort, not wealth and style. Avoid pine if your ideal customer expects a posh or high-tech environment.

- Cherry. This elegant wood choice has decorated the offices of the rich for centuries. It represents long-standing wealth, the ability to overcome economic hardships, and a strong masculine heritage. Cherry is not a good choice for business owners appealing to a primarily female market, as its masculine associations are too entrenched to ignore.

Maple

Oak

Teak

Pine

Cherry

Metal. Born from the industrial age, metal represents humankind's ability to mold and craft the earth's resources. Metal brings a sharp penetrating energy into a room. This can work well if the business provides products or services that eliminate anything excessive and focus on the essential. Metal is dense concentrated energy and can help you pull your thoughts together when you are feeling scattered. However, too much Metal energy will result in a sharp sarcastic tongue and biting wit. Metal-and-glass combinations are both sharp and volatile and should be avoided indoors. Metal-and-wood is an excellent combination. The metal brings definition, the wood brings strength. Metal can also work with a laminate top, but an entirely metal desk is cold and off-putting.

Metal energy is mental. It draws the body's chi force upward, aiding mental exertion and draining the physical body. If you do a lot of mental work, a partially metal desk is a good move, but avoid an all-metal chair. Your physical body will need the comfort and support of a wood or padded-leather chair if you are going to sit at a metal desk all day.

Materials behave differently in various combinations than they do in isolation. While metal and glass create a sharp precarious energy indoors, a laminate desktop such as this one blends harmoniously with the metal legs.

Glass. Glass is dramatic and can be stunning, but it is also revealing. A glass desktop indicates that you have nothing to hide, and its primary drawback is that you can hide nothing. Glass desktops do not have drawers or other supportive containers for holding onto things. As a result, things come and go quickly on a glass desk. If you have a glass desk and find that the movement or pace of your office is too quick, you can slow it down by placing a wooden hutch or woven accessory with small compartments on the top of the desk, giving yourself the ability to hold and contain the chi force there. In the very least, place a small potted plant on one corner of the desk to ground the chi.

Glass combines best with wood or laminate. Glass-on-metal or glass-on-glass are combinations too volatile and risky to be healthy for most businesses.

Use laminates to get creative, have fun, and customize your office, all while keeping costs down. If the artificial factor gets to be too much for you, incorporate playful or organic objects such as these gerbera daisies to bring you back into balance.

Laminate. Laminates are created by pressing thin layers together, and can have just about any look you can think of. Versatility is their strongest design feature, and lower cost ranks a close second. A laminate desk is energetically neutral. It does not drain the physical body or the brain, but simply holds things in place. Drawbacks include sharp edges (it is difficult to round a laminate desk), easy chipping, and lesser quality craftsmanship.

Sizes

For a long time, we have heard that bigger is better. Large imposing desks have always indicated that a powerful person works there. But desk size depends upon the size of the person seated, particularly the person's height and the length of their arms. Before you decide on a desk, sit down at it.

A typical office desk is 60 inches long and 30 inches deep. This desk size was adequate before we started putting computers on them. If you have a computer monitor on your desk, the preferred desk size for most people is 72 inches long and 36 inches deep. Desks larger than 72 inches by 36 inches make it difficult for most people to access all the areas of their desks without moving their seats.

A large desk connotes command over your business situation and power in the market place. However, if the desk is so large that you cannot reach the items at the back, you will lose your command over things. Select the smaller L-shaped desk to avoid this problem.

Once you are seated, make certain that the desk fits your frame in the following ways.

- Your feet should rest flat on the floor, and your thighs should be parallel to the floor, with enough room between the desk and the chair that you can easily slide under the desk.

- Your arms make a 90-degree angle when you rest your palms flat on the desk (wrists straight).

- You can reach the front of the desk while seated.

- You can reach to both ends of the desk while seated.

- The desk surface is large enough that you can easily unfold a newspaper on top of it.

Never underestimate the power of versatility in an office space. This teardrop-shaped table can provide additional working space for large projects, as well as become an instant conference table.

Small home desks. If your desk folds out of a large cabinet or tucks into a kitchen counter, chances are it is smaller than 60 inches by 30 inches. Oftentimes, these desk surfaces are as small as 30 inches by 18 inches. These small desks are typically cluttered, not because the people who work there are messy, but because they are too small for the need they are trying to serve. It is like taking four small children and crowding them into one bedroom; things are going to get chaotic.

If you are working from a small desk, limit the amount of things you do at that desk to avoid clutter build-up. A smaller surface can typically work as a mail center, a phone-message center, or a bill-paying center, but not all three. Your efforts are valued more when you ask for and receive a desk large enough to handle all the work you do.

Many businesses have been launched from the dining-room table. Although this surface can work as a desk, using it that way disrupts the family's equanimity, because it can no longer provide space for family dining, homework, or other family functions. You will feel torn between family responsibilities and work if you use the family dining table as your desk.

To "grow" a small space and make it as functional as possible, add containers. Just as closet organizers can triple the storage capacity of a closet, so too containers can triple how many materials your desk can effectively hold.

A U-shaped desk provides containment and a feeling of security. If you start feeling too contained, move the entire desk out about three inches from the wall. This will allow for more chi flow behind the desk area and reduce the tendency for the chi to stagnate.

Shapes

The shape of your desk needs to match the work you do there. We will look at variations on three general shapes—rectangles, circles, curves—and see how shape can affect work performance.

Rectangles. Rectangular desks are ideal for office work. This shape generates Earth energy, which supports the desk's function of grounding all the mental work that goes on there. Adding two rectangles together to form an L-shaped desk is another strong Earth-energy shape. The L-shaped desk has even stronger containment features than the single rectangle, since it wraps around the person's body and encourages them to stay seated.

If you have an L-shaped desk, position the L so that you have easy access to the entry point of the desk. If you make it too difficult to get in and out, you will resist going there and feel trapped while you are working.

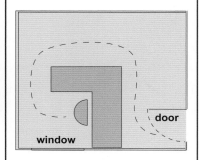

Drawing A
Poor positioning

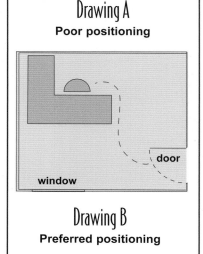

Drawing B
Preferred positioning

Nestled in the inside curve, this shapely desk will focus your energy on what is directly in front of you, helping you concentrate for longer periods of time. The conference table area has an outside curve that will keep people moving and stop visitors and coworkers from lingering.

Circles. Circular desks are too yang and will prevent the person seated there from being able to concentrate or remain seated for a long period of time. Use circular shapes for conference tables where you need to brainstorm creative solutions, but not for deskwork that requires concentration.

Curved shapes. Relatively new, the crescent-shaped desk works well for people who need to concentrate, since they sit inside the curve. With a curved shape, energy pulls inward, seeking the center. If you are seated at that center point, the shape will pull your energy in, concentrating it and creating density. This will aid your attempts to focus and sustain mental efforts for a longer period of time. The U-shaped desk is an extreme example of the crescent. With longer arms that wrap around the person, a U-shaped desk can feel stifling to some, comforting to others. It depends on how much containment you feel comfortable with. If you tend to get claustrophobic in an elevator, you will want to avoid a U-shaped desk.

Closed front vs. open front

The primary feng shui concern is whether the front of your desk is open or closed. An open desk, such as a table, allows the client to see the part of your body that is seated. This desk style will bring you into more intimate contact with anyone seated across the desk. They will automatically feel more connected to you. This desk style works well if you counsel clients or resolve employee concerns while seated at your desk. A closed front will keep your energy separate from your client's energy, and will also separate you more from employees. This type of desk is typically seen in an executive's office, where separation is associated with rank. In this case, the closed front is a sign of respect for that position.

When selecting your desk style, decide just how "available" you want to be to your clients. If you find clients are too invasive (calling you at home or on weekends), you can increase formality and a degree of separation by selecting a closed-front desk. If your clients find you distant or impersonal, you should consider an open-front desk.

A closed front, such as this one, provides a degree of separation between you and your client. If you could benefit from stronger boundaries between yourself and clients (or your co-workers) consider a closed-front desk.

Color

The color of your desk will determine how your energy moves while seated there. Use the following Desk Color Chart to select a desk color that will increase the pattern you need to do your best work.

You can balance the effect of your desk color by the objects you place on the desktop. For example, you could place a green plant on a black desk, bringing the vibration of green into your immediate work environment.

Desk color chart

Desk color	Energy pattern
Black	Moves energy down and in, encourages introspection, opens up possibilities
Brown	Supports and strengthens the physical body, does not activate the mind
White	Energizes the mind, drains the physical body
Gray	Focuses the mind, drains the physical body
Green	Balances between body and mind, sustains longer efforts
Muted tones	Increase mental focus without draining the physical body as much as straight gray
Bright colors	Activate the eye, making the body and mind restless

When selecting a primarily grayed color scheme, make certain to punctuate this subdued energy with color accents.

The intensity of the colors in this cabinet help vitalize an otherwise austere setting.

For grounding and stability, this office incorporated a muted color scheme. Browns and other earth tones support the physical body rather than the mind.

Adding white to an office creates clarity and mental focus.

Selecting the right chair

When you shop for the perfect feng shui chair, sit in it, then consider whether it fits the following criteria.

Back support. Your chair should fit your back like your shoes fit your feet. In order to be at your best, both physically and mentally, you need to be supported. For the Chinese, back support is vital. As the turtle's shell keeps it from harm and protects it from the elements, so the back of your desk chair should provide consistent support. The chair back should be high enough that it supports the upper, as well as the lower back and fits the contours of your back.

Although you give up back support, this "perch" chair offers other enticements. You can sit sideways, using the top support as an armrest, or sit backward, straddling the chair as you would a bar stool. This new position might just generate new ways of thinking and provide you with novel solutions to old problems.

This funky office chair is made from bungee cords. The elastic bands across the back and seat are surprisingly supportive and energizing at the same time. For additional lumbar support, use a small pillow.

Arm support. Secondary to back support, arm support allows you to relax periodically throughout the day, which keeps your overall energy levels up. Armrests can make you feel hemmed in, however, as they keep your arms close to your body. If you desire more freedom on the job, consider a chair without armrests. (Because metal armrests are usually colder than body temperature, they can be particularly uncomfortable. Placing your elbows on cold metal armrests can startle and unsettle you.)

Wheels. Freedom of movement is closely associated with freedom of expression. Make certain your chair can move freely from one end of your desk area to the other.

Materials. Select your chair material in combination with your desk. For example, if you already have a metal desk, you probably do not need more Metal energy. Consider a leather or wooden chair instead. On the other hand, if your entire desk is wood, you can add metal to your chair, since Metal energy increases mental focus. Be certain to mix a glass desktop with either a leather or wooden chair, rather than a metal chair.

Height. The height of the chair depends on the height of your body. Test your chair height by sitting in the chair and placing your hands on the desk in front of you. The right chair height will leave your arms at a 90-degree angle, with your wrists flat. This will eliminate any unnecessary strain on your wrists and help prevent carpal tunnel syndrome. Your feet should rest flat on the floor, and your thighs should be parallel to the floor, with enough room between the desk and the chair that you can slide easily under the desk.

Reclining chairs. Leaning back in your chair puts the left side of the brain on hold, encouraging imagination and creativity. If you need to draw from the right side of your brain in your work, make certain you get a chair that reclines.

The good feng shui chair (such as this one) allows the owner to adjust back support, arm support, seat height, and seat depth. This chair also allows body heat to release out the back to maintain a comfortable body temperature.

These leather chairs aid this sales manager in convincing clients to make a purchase. Leather enhances fire energy, which fans people's passions, focuses their attention on the needs of the moment, and generates an expansive energy pattern conducive to spending.

Eye levels

Although what you place on your wall is important, where you place it also holds significance. Where something is at on the wall affects which part of your brain is triggered when you look at it. Here feng shui finally meets up with modern brain research. Scientists have discovered that eye movements trigger neural responses in different areas of the brain, depending on how high the eye is looking.

Above your head. Items above your head jump-start your imagination. This is the realm of the possible, the imaginable, the achievable. Traditional feng shui advice is to place items above your head that you want to move into your reality in the future. This is a great place to post mission statements or work goals, but placing too much up high will create a stronger tendency to daydream. The more activity there is up high, the stronger your grounding needs to be.

Eye level. When you look straight ahead—eye level— your brain stays in present time. Feng shui advises that whatever is directly in front of you on the wall (eye level), influences how you react and respond to events in present time. Keep in mind that, in your office, you will often be seated. Therefore, hanging a piece of wall art so that it is eye level while you are seated will keep you in present time during your work day. If, while you are seated, you constantly look up to view something that is eye level at standing height, you will be more likely to imagine future events, daydream, and entertain possible scenarios.

The floor. When you look down at your feet or at items on the floor, your brain moves into past-time events more easily. According to feng shui, what is on your floor represents how the energy of your past is still impacting your present. This could be former clients, unresolved work issues, or even nonwork-related family issues that originated in the past and that you keep dragging forward into your present, trying to coax yourself into resolution.

Items, such as this lintel, should be placed above eye level to energize any future projects.

Allowing items to build up on the floor will keep your energy stuck in past time, making it harder to be present in the moment.

Arranging your work space

Although each space contains its own mysteries and quirks, there are certain rules of arrangement that apply to most work spaces, most of the time. Once you learn the rules, you will be in a better position to understand when and how to apply them, as well as when it is okay to break them.

Placing your desk

Your desk is the most important placement you will make in your office. If you set up your desk correctly, it can provide support, opportunities, and inspiration for all that you do.

To provide the best possible desk placement, make certain it is out of the chi flow of the door, that you have a wall to one side and solid wall behind you, and that you can see people coming and going.

The command position. A most important thing to consider when placing your desk is how to set yourself up in the room's command position.

The command position has four components:

- It provides a view of the door. You will feel more secure and in control of your situation when you are able to see who is coming. A view of the door also indicates the ability to respond proactively.

- It is out of the mouth of chi. The energy in a doorway is volatile. Sitting too closely to this type of volatile energy will make it more difficult for you to focus and remain centered.

- It places a solid wall behind you. The "energy centers" in the back (referred to in the Vedic system as charkas) move fields of energy throughout your body. By protecting your back, you protect these centers and allow for a smooth, uninhibited flow of energy throughout your entire system.

- It places a wall to one side of you, if possible. You feel more comfortable in a workspace if there is a wall to one side. Even though your peripheral vision can take in what is happening 180 degrees around you, it is difficult to feel in real control of such a wide angle without constantly turning your head from side to side. With a wall on one side, you only have to manage a 90-degree angle.

Before feng shui: This graphic designer worked with her back to the door, unable to see who was coming and going behind her.

After feng shui: By turning her desk to face the door, she gave herself visual and energetic command over her entire workspace.

The following adjustments will show you how to use the command position to select the best possible desk placement.

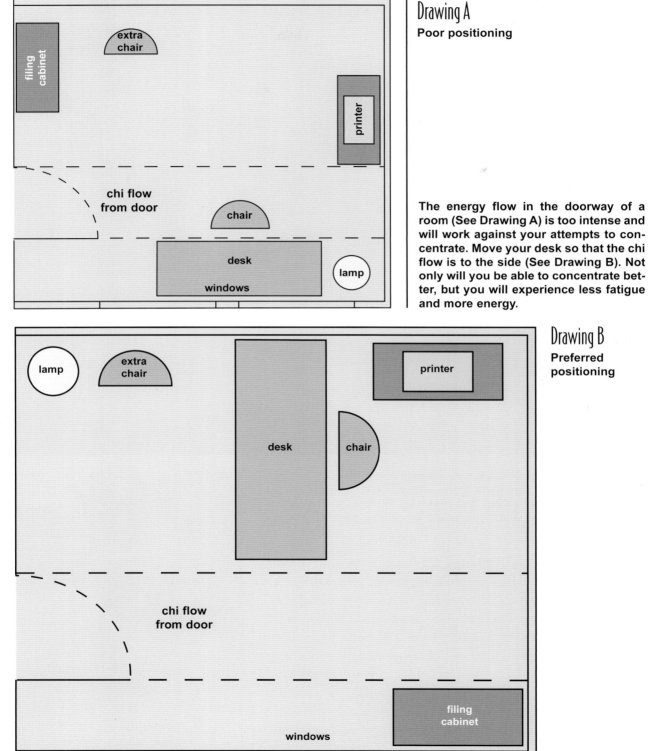

Drawing A
Poor positioning

The energy flow in the doorway of a room (See Drawing A) is too intense and will work against your attempts to concentrate. Move your desk so that the chi flow is to the side (See Drawing B). Not only will you be able to concentrate better, but you will experience less fatigue and more energy.

Drawing B
Preferred positioning

If you cannot turn your desk, use a small convex mirror, like the type you find at an auto parts store, and attach it so that you can view the area behind you. Because the surface is convex, a three-inch mirror will allow you to see more area than a four-foot flat mirror would.

Face your guests. Your empowerment can come from simply turning your desk to face people as they enter your work area. When they are able to enter your space at your back, they intuit that you are in a subordinate position to themselves. If you can turn to face them as they enter, this helps to level the playing field. If you are in a cubicle environment where it is impossible to move your desk, consider moving where your doorway is (those panels can be moved) or placing a convex mirror on your monitor so that you can still see people coming up behind you. It will support your chi and help you interact with them from a more powerful position.

A commanding view. Sit down at your desk and look around. The view that greets you when you sit down to work will affect everything that you do at your desk. Although some people are better than others at blocking out what is in their visual range, it still takes energy to ignore your surroundings. There are three important considerations with regard to the commanding view.

- A blank wall. Try to avoid having a blank wall closer than eight feet in front of you. A blank wall indicates lack of vision, perception, and opportunities. Cover your wall with an empowering view—one that inspires you, helps you feel good about yourself and your potential, and lifts your spirits.

This desk placement provides more than just a stunning view. With a supportive wall at the back and a cubicle wall that wraps around one side, this placement offers the person seated at the desk visual command of everything that happens in the office.

Avoiding poison arrows. After determining where your command position is, check this area for "poison arrows." The term "poison arrow" refers to an edge (such as the corner of a wall or a filing cabinet with sharp edges) that is sharp enough to project an intense line of energy outward from the point where the two sides come together.

To reduce the effect of a poison arrow, paint both sides of the arrow the same color, preferably an earth hue such as this gold. For additional buffering, place a plant or dispersing object between the desk and the corner.

If you position your body within the trajectory of this energetic line, it has a slicing quality that undermines your physical strength and weakens your immune system. Traditionally, poison arrows represented sabotage, either self-sabotage or the sabotaging efforts of other people.

If you find a poison arrow, try to move the piece of furniture so that you can keep your desk in the command position.

If you cannot move the furniture or the wall, you have two options.

- You can buffer the sharp edge by placing a plant, a crystal, or some other diffusing object between the edge and your body.

- You can move your desk.

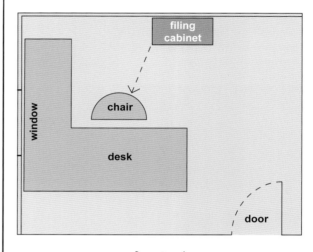

Drawing A
Poor positioning
Edge of filing cabinet creates a poison arrow.

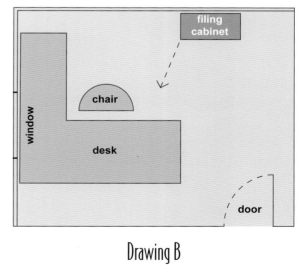

Drawing B
Preferred positioning
Poison arrow no longer intersects with the back of the chair.

Create your own focal point by installing a fabric screen. This fabric partial wall provides privacy and increases focus by reducing the visual scope of the workstation from 180 degrees to 90 degrees. To make certain the fabric generates and energy that supports you, pick out your own fabric from the fabric store and use it to cover a generic cubical panel.

■ If your walls are a ways away, you will need to focus your gaze on something that is closer than your walls. Consider installing a partial wall or screen.

■ Another disrupting visual influence is a chaotic view. If the scene outside your window is of tractors tearing up the street for weeks on end, that vision of chaos will find its way into your thinking patterns, your work performance, and your interactions with others. Protect yourself from such chi disruptions by blocking off the chaos, using window coverings, a folding screen, or a plant.

This office uses stained glass to transform a view of the neighboring concrete building into a work of art.

Working with the midline. Starting from your doorway, the midline of your office is at the halfway point. Once someone crosses this midline, they have moved from the public area of your office to the private area. You can use this distinction between public and private areas to send a message to your clients and/or employees.

If you place your desk in front of the midline, so that your seat is in the front half of the room, you send the message that you are accessible approachable, and desire more informal interactions.

If you place your desk so that your seat is behind the midline, you send the message that you expect those who enter to respect your privacy, that you are available only under certain conditions, and that you desire their interactions with you to be according to certain guidelines or office protocol.

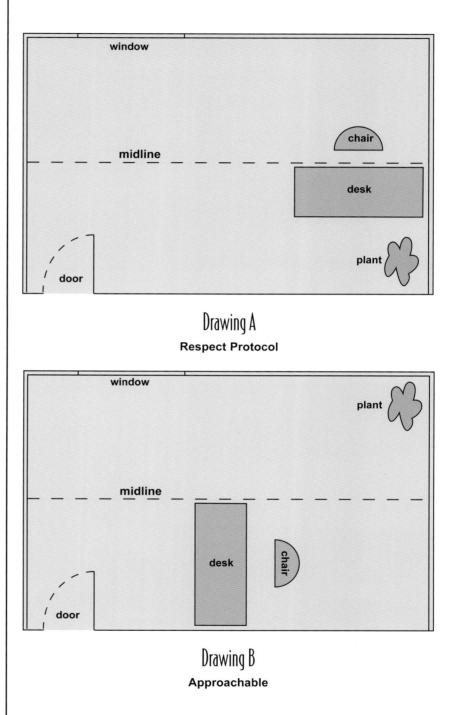

Drawing A
Respect Protocol

Drawing B
Approachable

Using plants. When faced with an unusual office shape, use plants to fill out odd angles or corners, making the space as rectangular as possible.

By filling this corner in with a large plant, the space behind the desk evens out and supports the back of the person seated at the desk.

The office above has a sharply angled corner directly behind the desk.

Ba gua "map" your office

Before placing items in your office, perform a feng shui analysis called "ba gua mapping." The ba gua is a template that describes how your physical environment relates to and affects various aspects of your life. Divided into eight sectors surrounding a center (the word ba gua literally means "eight sectors"), the ba gua provides a pattern for balanced energy through an entire life cycle. By arranging items in your office according to this model, you can generate a balanced flow of energy in your business as well. If you are experiencing specific problems in any of the areas represented by a ba gua sector, feng shui recommends making adjustments to the corresponding areas of your office.

The ba gua life cycle. The sectors of the ba gua relate to the trigrams of the *I Ching,* the Oriental philosophy book commonly known as *The Book of Changes,* discussed in chapters 3–10 of this book. The arrangement of trigrams depicted below (known as the King Wen Model) is a cyclical arrangement, showing how the rhythms in nature, such as the changing seasons and the hours of the day, represent the changing nature of all things. Starting at the top and moving clockwise, the trigrams at the cardinal points stand for summer, fall, winter, and spring. The trigrams in between each of the cardinal points represent times of transition between seasons. These different qualities were thought to be the building blocks of all life, and their position in relationship to each other depicted how life progressed through predictable phases. The Ba Gua Map for Businesses on page 35 illustrates some of the primary characteristics of each sector (or gua) and how these guas relate to the world of business. (For detailed information on the eight guas, see chapters 3–10.)

King Wen model

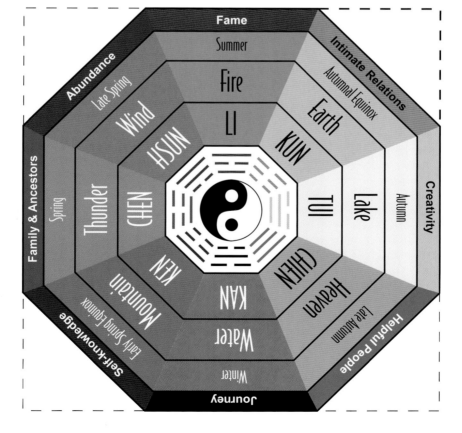

Ba gua map for businesses

Abundance/wind ☴

This represents your external expression of your internal gifts. True and generous expression of these gifts will bring prosperity.
Colors: Purple, green
Shapes: Vertical columns and pillars, random patterns
Symbols: Wood, wind, sky, airplanes, frogs, coins, sailing ships, treasure chests, chimes
Business symbol: Financial controls, cash flow, profitability

Fame/fire ☲

This gua is your reputation—how your clients and other businesses perceive you and respond to your business.
Colors: Red, orange, neon
Shapes: Star shapes, sunbursts, triangles, pyramids, diamonds
Symbols: Fire, sun, stars, phoenix, birds, animals, leather, candles, incense, scents
Business symbol: Reputation, goodwill, market share

Intimate Relations/earth ☷

This area is concerned with how trustworthy and trusting you are. Trust enables you to form lasting relationships that are mutually supportive.
Colors: Pink, taupe, tan, beige, off-whites
Shapes: Horizontal shapes and lines, rectangles and squares, the horizon
Symbols: Earth, soft nurturing items, hollow (receptive) items, pillows, padded furniture, containers, quan yin, precious stones
Business symbol: Employee longevity, partnering businesses, partners

Family and Ancestors/thunder ☳

This is your connection to the past and your ability to grow from the experiences, innovations, and limitations of others.
Color: Spring green
Shapes: Tall vertical shapes, columns, pillars
Symbols: Wood, dragons, growing things, plants, columns, sound energy, items from the past, stripes, vertical rectangles
Business symbol: Initial funding and support from others, business plan and resulting loan

Health/tai chi ☯

The center is not a trigram but represents the eye of the hurricane, the balancing force amidst constant change and interaction.
Colors: Yellow, gold
Shapes: The cross, any shape with four corners, a center in any other shape
Symbols: Earth, the medium through which other things travel and transform, containers, open space
Business symbol: The industry itself

Creativity/lake ☱

This area represents your relationship to fullness, your response to scarcity, and your satisfaction in a job well done.
Colors: White, rainbow colors
Shapes: Arcs, circles, droplets
Symbols: Metal, tiger, round items, rainbows, toys, art, goblet (chalice), luxurious excess, open containers, vacations
Business symbol: Sunsetting products, return on investment, retirement, exit strategies

Self-knowledge/mountain ☶

This is the point of individuation—how your chosen path sets itself apart from other paths.
Colors: Blue, brown
Shapes: Horizontal earth shapes, rectangle, squares
Symbols: Earth, pottery, clay, mountain, books, containers, foundations, large heavy objects, Buddhas, bodies of wisdom
Business symbol: Logo, business name, other identity symbols

Journey/water ☵

This is your decision about what business or career to pursue. This phase encourages you to dig deep to find your true gifts.
Colors: Black, deep blues
Shapes: Flowing organic shapes, cascading items
Symbols: Water, turtles, terraces, glass, mirrors, flowing shapes, hanging items, hanging plants
Business symbol: Mission statement, statement of purpose

Helpful People/heaven ☰

This is a time for refinement, for letting go of all the clients and projects that no longer serve you, and for living your essence fully.
Colors: White, silver, gray
Shapes: Arcs, circles, cutaways, sharp angles
Symbols: Metal, tools for cutting and refining, travel, community symbols, mentors, angels and spirit guides
Business symbol: Assessment/restructuring of business to match new goals, a strong well-defined brand

Placing the map on your floor plan. Begin with a floor plan of your office or building. If you do not have a floor plan, draw one to scale that includes windows, walls, and doors. Look at the general shape of the floor plan. Draw a rectangle over the floor plan, cutting off areas that jut out and enclosing areas that indent. The general rule to apply when deciding whether something is a "missing sector" (indented area) or an extension (jut out) is to look at whether the existing space is more than half of the width or length of the room. If what is there is half or more than half, draw your rectangle to include that area. If what is there is less than half, draw your rectangle to exclude that area. See the sample floor plans below.

Once you know which areas of your office relate to different sectors of the ba gua, examine each area to see what general message you are sending yourself about that aspect of your work life. The following information will guide you in reviewing each ba gua sector and in making conscious choices about where to place items such as your trash can or your spouse's photograph.

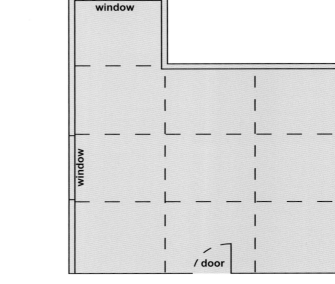

Abundance	window Fame	Intimate Relations
window Family & Ancestors	Health	Creativity
Self-knowledge	Journey / door	Helpful People

Regular office shape: no extensions or missing sectors

Office shape with extension in Abundance sector

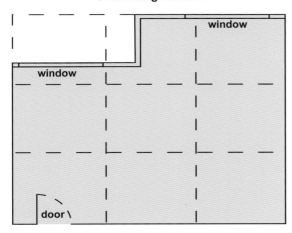

Office shape missing part of Abundance and Fame sectors

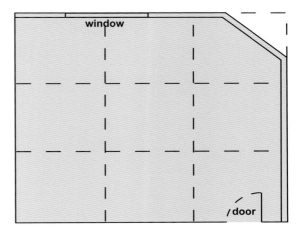

Office shape missing part of Intimate Relations sector

I Ching trigrams

Each gua sector is referred to here with its I Ching trigram association. This will help you cross-reference the information in this section with chapters 3–10 on the I Ching.

 KAN

Journey/water. Often the doorway into the office, the Journey gua is concerned with whether or not you are on the right path. At the foundation of this sector is the belief that life is meaningful and has purpose. As an extension of that belief, the only business that holds the power to deeply satisfy you is one that allows you to express your true essence and fulfill your life's purpose.

Reflective surfaces, including windowpanes, are ideal for the Kan trigram. They represent the reflective quality of a deep pool of water, without adding actual water to the space.

Items to include in this area:

- Purpose. Make certain there is a purpose for everything you have placed in this area. Items without a home, papers without files, or the oddball item that does not fit should not be located here.

- Oceans. If you feel that you have not yet found your purpose, place a picture of the ocean or a star-filled sky in this area. Both represent your connection to the cosmic order of which you are a part.

- Turtles. If you feel you have found your purpose and want to progress along your journey, place a turtle in this area. Turtles mean that you have aligned with cosmic forces and are ready to create a new life.

- Quan Yin. If you desire more inner peace over the issue of purpose, place a Quan Yin statue in this area. Quan Yin is the female goddess of peace and compassion, and placing her in the Journey gua represents your willingness to fulfill your purpose.

Items to avoid in this area are:

- bright colors and patterns,
- stormy pictures,
- too many electronics.

☰ KEN

Self-knowledge/mountain. A great place for your desk or a reading chair, the Mountain gua represents your personal strength, self-mastery, and resourcefulness.

This blessing rock was made with granite from the Wasatch mountain range and coconut fibers from Hawaii. To make your own blessing rock, braid your twine and then soak it for 2–3 hours. Wrap the twine around the rock as tightly as possible (the length of the twine depends on the size of the rock). Place the rock in the sun. As the twine dries, it will tighten even more around your rock.

A built-in bookshelf is ideal in the Ken (Self-knowledge) area of the ba gua, as this area relates to self-awareness and wisdom.

Items to include in this area:

- Mountain. Hanging a picture of a mountain here represents inner stillness and your ability to "stand firm" in the face of difficulty.

- Books and journals. Studying and gaining knowledge is a primary way of coming to understand the human condition. The Chinese consider the pursuit of wisdom to be a lifelong challenge.

- Large heavy objects. Large heavy objects help ground and stabilize this area, connoting strength and endurance. This could be as simple as placing a paperweight on your desk, or as major as erecting a statue. If your desk is here, make certain it is sturdy.

- Photograph of self. Since this area is about knowing and controlling the self, a photograph of you at your best will constantly remind you of what kind of person you desire to be.

Items to avoid in this area are:

- running water,
- moving objects,
- symbols of weakness.

 # CHEN

Family and Ancestors/thunder. This area of the ba gua represents your ability to accept support and help from others. Whether this help comes in the form of a bank loan, a new assistant, or simply the right consultant, you can encourage or block it here.

Items to include in this area:

- Healthy plants. Plant life supports human life and is a powerful symbol of how we are all interconnected.

- Dragons. Representing the breath of life, the dragon vitalizes everything it encounters. It is typically associated with the east and the rising sun.

- Tall vertical objects. Pillars, lamps, or columns link heaven and earth together, representing strong support for your efforts.

- Supportive people. Place pictures of supportive friends and family members here, reminding yourself that no one goes through this life experience untouched by others.

Items to avoid in this area are:

- single items,

- sharp cutting items,

- notices of rejection.

Want your employees to support each other? Let them play together. This vertical pillar constructed from colored cards supplies creative play for a cross-functional team. Placing the pillar in the center of the team environment also indicates where each member's personal workspace ends and the cocreative space begins.

 # HSUN

Abundance/wind. This area of the ba gua represents the opportunities that come your way, as well as your ability to take advantage of those opportunities when they come. Welcome an abundance of opportunities to your business by activating the energy of this area.

A playful depiction of this client's financial goals, the one-million dollar bill is proudly displayed in the Abundance area of the office.

Items to include in this area:

- Moving objects. Those moving objects you needed to remove from the Self-knowledge gua are perfect here. The Abundance gua is activated by movement (symbolic of the wind through the trees).

- Paper money or coins. If you would like your opportunities to result in increased cash flow, place actual money in this area. (Be certain to use large denomination bills, I Ching coins, or gold dollars, no pocket change, please.)

- Bamboo. Bamboo grows quickly and is resilient. Because it is available to everyone in China, rich and poor alike, it represents the ability to make your own opportunities.

- Jade plant. Although any tall standing plant is also a good choice, jade plants are especially prized in this area because their leaves are the shape of coins.

Items to avoid in this area are:

- trash can,

- bills or overdue accounts,

- long-term storage.

Keep the energy moving in the Abundance (rear-left corner) area of your desk by placing a small fan there. The blowing fan awakens Wind, a messenger from the heavens who whispers of fortuitous opportunities.

 LI

Fame/fire. This area represents how you are perceived by others. This can include your coworkers, colleagues, employees, clients, and other businesses. Include items here that represent your vision of success.

Although any candle will enhance the Fire energy needed in the Fame sector, the dancing butterflies depicted on this candle introduce an additional element of transformation. If you want to completely transform your relationship with the external world, use butterflies.

Items to include in this area:

- Lighting. A great place for a lamp, especially a torchère. Increased lighting in general increases yang movement, the upward expanding energy of Fire.

- Color. Here is where you can hang that painting with the intense color or crazy patterns. Items that represent things you are passionate about work well here, too.

- Expansion. Clear things out of your way so that you have some room to move around in this area. Use windows, mirrors, or a large landscape painting to give yourself the feeling of expansion.

- Accomplishments. Display items that represent something you are proud of or something that you worked hard to accomplish.

- Social connections. We all enjoy socializing in different ways. Display something here that represents how you like to socialize.

Items to avoid in this area are:

- heavy items or clutter,
- dark rooms,
- water.

 KUN

42

Intimate Relations/earth. This area is concerned with relationships that last over time. In setting up this part of your office, consider who the people are that you would like to have a lasting relationship with. These people can be clients, employees, business partners, or supportive businesses.

Conference areas need to "contain" clients. A conference table in the middle of an open room does not provide enough containment to help clients feel safe. This partial wall creates a semienclosed conference area, providing safety for clients while keeping costs under control.

Items to include in this area:

- Hardwoods. Anything made from oak or another long-lasting hardwood. If your furniture is built to last, your business has a better chance of lasting.

- Containers. When you keep energy around for awhile, you need a container for it or your office will become chaotic. The right containers will keep the office running smoothly and the clutter problem at a minimum.

- Objects you value. By placing objects that you value highly in this area, you set your intention to focus on the value of long-lasting trustworthy relationships. The underlying belief in this concept is that what you focus your energy on is what you tend to discover, time and again, in the world around you.

- Seating area. This is a great place to sit down and converse with clients and employees alike, if you want them to feel that they can trust you and are trusted by you.

Items to avoid in this area are:
- trash,
- disposables,
- mobiles or wind chimes.

 TUI

Creativity/lake. This area concerns itself with how you spend all the abundance and fullness that you drew to you in the Abundance gua. Your relationship with the earth's fullness controls whether you experience the world around you as one of "lack" or one of "plenty." To see and experience the world's plenty, is to find the joy of this gua.

This stained-glass quilt is an exquisite example of how you can bring all the colors of the rainbow into your office. The rippled glass used for the background layer shimmers like a virtual lake when caught by the sun's rays.

Items to include in this area:

- Your budgets. Get your budget under control by facing your spending tendencies on a daily basis. Since this area holds the pattern in place for how you respond to an overflow or lack of money, it is the best place to initiate a new pattern, whatever you want that new pattern to be.

- Gemstones and geodes. Include items made from the earth in their raw state (geodes, uncut crystals, gemstones.)

- Rainbows. Whether you incorporate rainbows through pictures, a dyed cloth, or leaded-glass panes on your window, rainbow rays will remind you of the earth's fullness through one of the most joyful and creative of all mediums—color.

- Photocopiers. Since this area relates to the earth's fecundity, a photocopier is a great way of making more out of what you currently have.

Items to avoid in this area are:

- sparseness,
- evidence of destructive patterns,
- empty containers.

 CHIEN

Helpful People/heaven. Dedicated to refinement and letting go, this gua is where you get to release everything that is not working for you. This includes clients, procedures, product lines, and employees. Whatever you want to shift out of your experience, bring it into this area.

44

When bookshelves are crammed to capacity, it represents over-whelm and overextension in a business. To attract new clients or projects to your business, streamline your shelves.

Leaving open space in your shelves indicates a comfortable balance between yin (the force that makes us hold on to things) and yang (the force that encourages us to let it all go).

Items to include in this area:

- Trash can. Yep, here is where you can place your trash can, as well as your shredder, and any other tools of elimination.

- Filing cabinets. Bringing order to what you have is key in deciding what you are going to keep and what you are going to give away. Metal filing cabinets are especially powerful for refining, since metal creates a sharp cutting energy.

- Metal items. Anything made from metal, including lamps, picture frames, tables, or chairs will bring refinement to this gua.

- Tools for sorting. Whether your sorting tools include employee evaluations or manila file folders, this is a great place to make decisions of discernment.

Items to avoid in this area are:

- long-term storage,
- clutter and piles,
- items representing compromise.

Priority placements in your office

Where you place things depends upon how often you use them. As explained in *Feng Shui Living*, priority placement feng shui arranges an environment based on ease of use. To apply priority placements to an office, the following guidelines should help.

Priority-one office areas. Priority-one office areas are those areas within your reach and immediate visual range while you are seated at your desk. When setting up your office, place the items needed to perform daily tasks in priority-one areas. For example, your computer, phone, day planner, and printer should all be within your reach while you are seated at your desk. A less obvious example of using priority-one placements might be where you display your financial reports. To gain more control over the financial situation of your business, place your financial reports in a location where you see them every day (a bulletin board to the side of your computer screen works well). Not allowing this information to slip out of consciousness will support you in developing a more controlled relationship with your business's finances. My clients have found that they pay fewer late charges and have fewer cash-flow surprises when they post their accounts payable and profit/loss statements where they can see them every day.

To make full use of your priority-one areas, create a daily activity chart that lists your daily tasks. The Daily Activity Chart for Priority-one Areas on page 46 will help you set up your office to optimize your efforts and help you prioritize how you spend your time. Make certain your daily chart matches the activities that would best support your business.

By gathering everything you need for your work into a single container, you simplify the daily task of gathering your tools. This feng shui consultant packs her leather bag with multiple items needed for her work. If she were to repack each time, it would add thirty minutes to her prep time.

Daily activity chart for priority-one areas

Activity	Item(s) needed	Placement of item(s)
Answer phones within three rings. Return phone messages within 24 hours.	Phone, phone message pad, day planner, client files, vertical-stacking file holder	Place phone on right rear of desktop, phone message pad in front of phone, and day planner on the right-front corner of desktop. Place active and new-client file folders in vertical-stacking file holder on desktop.
Read and respond to e-mail within 24 hours.	Computer with e-mail, day planner	Place printout of updated client information in day planner. Place day planner on right-front corner of the desktop. Place computer on left-rear corner of desktop.
Schedule with clients. While scheduling, make note of address changes and other client information.	Computer with e-mail, phone, day planner, active client file folders, vertical-stacking file holder	Place day planner on right-front corner and computer on the left-rear corner of desktop. Place phone on right-rear corner of the desktop. Place active and new-client file folders in vertical-stacking file holder on left side of desktop.
Perform two 2-hour client consultations.	Tape measure, graph paper, write-up template, client folder, resource catalogs, I Ching coins, red envelopes, small mirrors (eight-sided, concave, and convex), ruler or scale, paint color fan decks, ba gua map, five-element charts, and questionnaires	Place all items necessary for consulting into one consultation briefcase. Place briefcase between the desk and the office door where you can grab it quickly as you walk out.
Review financials and access current situation. Track any money spent and balance checkbook.	Weekly profit/loss report, checkbook registrar, receipts for any tax-deductible expenses, file for receipts, vertical-stacking file holder	Post weekly profit/loss and bank account printouts on bulletin board at left of desk. Keep checkbook register out and visible on left side of desk. Keep file folder for tax-deductible expenses in vertical-stacking file holder on desktop.
Record mileage from consulting.	Mileage record in day planner	Take day planner with you on consultations.
Centralize notes from consultations, client-needs lists, on-going project information, and mail requiring a response into in-box.	In-box that can hold up to one week of client information and mail	Place in-box on left-front corner of desktop next to vertical-stacking file holder.

Priority-two office areas. Priority-two office areas are places that are easy to access, but that you cannot reach from your desk. This includes a filing cabinet across the room or a bookshelf more than three feet away. For those office tasks that come up once a week, use priority-two areas. Do you have reference books that you need to look at or files to which you need regular access? If you do, place these books and filing cabinets in a priority-two zone. It will require more effort to get up and walk across the room to perform these tasks, but it will be more likely to happen if these items are not hidden away in a closet or stored in another room.

Priority-two areas should serve activities that you perform on either a weekly and a monthly basis. Create an activity chart for your weekly and monthly activities and use the Weekly Activity Chart for Priority-two Areas on page 48 and the Monthly Activity Chart for Priority-two Areas on page 49 to guide your placement of items in your office space.

This desk provides both priority-one and priority-two storage areas. The open book shelf and bulletin board keep items visible and within reach of the person seated at the desk. The book closet on the right allows you to tuck items out of view by closing the door. Keep pressing tasks visible and store reference materials behind closed doors.

Weekly activity chart for priority-two areas

Activity	Item(s) needed	Placement of item(s)
Send out information to prospective clients.	Informational brochures, stamps, access to e-mail, print-out of updated client information or on-line view of client information stored in computer	Place brochures and mailing supplies together in office supply cupboard across the room from your desk. Place day planner with updated client print-out on desktop.
Sort through in-box. Handle mail requiring a response. File client information in client folders to use for write-ups. Review on-going project needs.	In-box, active client and project files, vertical-stacking file holder, long-term files, filing cabinet	In-box and vertical-stacking file holder are on desktop. Place folders in file holder. Place inactive files for long-term clients or project information in filing cabinet across the room.
Shop for clients.	In-box, client-needs lists from client notes, active client files, vertical-stacking file holder	Place client notes in active client folders. Place folders in vertical-stacking file holder. Client notes are in in-box on desktop.
Complete write-ups for consultations.	Digital photos, computer with digital-imaging and word-processing software, notes from consultation, books for required research	Place digital camera on shelf by office door. Place research books on bookshelf on other side of office. Computer is on desktop.
Follow-up with previous clients. Work on on-going projects.	Long-term client files, long-term project files	Place inactive files for long-term clients and projects in filing cabinet across the room.
Turn new clients into long-term clients by creating permanent files for them.	Office supplies (e.g. manila folders, file holders, labeler), client notes from phone message pad and consultations	Place office supplies in designated cupboard across the room. Client notes are in in-box on desktop. Notes from phone calls are on phone message pad on the desktop.
Enter new client information in tickler system (automated reminder system for client follow-up).	Tickler system on computer	Computer is on desktop.
Pay accounts due and generate invoices for accounts payable. Get invoices ready to mail.	Computer with accounting software, accounts due/accounts payable printouts, client invoice and addresses, envelopes, stamps	Computer is on desktop. Client information is in vertical-stacking file holder on desktop. Place mailing supplies in office supply cupboard across the room.

Monthly activity chart for priority-two areas

Activity	Item(s) needed	Placement of item(s)
Generate and review monthly profit/loss report.	Accounting software in computer	Computer is on desktop.
Mail out reminders for overdue accounts.	Accounting software in computer, client addresses, envelopes, stamps	Computer is on desktop. Client information is in active files on desktop. Place mailing supplies in office supply cupboard across the room.
Review mission statement and recalibrate (if necessary) to achieve objectives.	Printout of mission statement, list of associated objectives	Frame mission statement and hang it above eye level on the wall in the Journey sector of your office. Post list of objectives next to mission statement.
Move client files that will not be active for the next six months from vertical-stacking file holder to long-term files.	Active files, file holders, labeler, long-term filing cabinet	Place inactive files in long-term filing cabinet across the room. Place office supplies in designated cupboard across the room.

This efficient office provides three levels of file storage.

- Priority-three files are across the room in a shared, long-term filing cabinet.

- Priority-two files are in handy filing areas stationed next to each desk.

- Active files are kept in the single file drawer, mounted on rollers for increased mobility.

Priority-three office areas. Priority-three areas are more remote (a closet, another room, the basement, off-site storage areas) and should house items that are required only once or twice throughout the year. For businesses, these areas typically include items for yearly employee reviews, tax information files, client files that have not been active for over a year, and resource materials that are not often used. Because these areas are remote, they require more effort to access. Filing problems can build up if the previous year's files have not been placed in a priority-three office area. This buildup can hamper your productivity and your ability to attract new business because your office contributes to a daily feeling of deluge.

A great time to move items into long-term areas is mid April, right after you finish your personal taxes (corporate taxes are due in March, so everything should be ready to file by mid April). This time of year is already a time of evaluation and assessment, cleaning up any errors or issues from the past, and making preparations for new energy to come into the business. Using the Yearly Activity Chart for Priority-three Areas on page 51, reward yourself after tax time by physically clearing out of your immediate environment any "past-time" files, clients, and projects that you do not want to give your energy to in the coming year.

For long-term storage, nothing tops this moveable filing system. The walls of files can be moved with either the turn of a crank or the touch of a button, allowing access to the files while conserving a tremendous amount of space.

Yearly activity chart for priority-three areas

Activity	Item(s) needed	Placement of item(s)
Store tax information.	W-2 forms, copies of tax returns, all receipts for previous year, client files, file-storage boxes	Previous year's tax information is in priority-two filing cabinet. Place this information in storage box and take to priority-three area.
Store inactive client information.	Client files, file-storage boxes	Previous year's client information is in priority-two filing cabinet. Place this information in storage box and take to priority-three area.
Store research and project information that has not been used within a year.	Research materials, project materials, file-storage boxes	Place outdated project information or research in storage box and take to priority-three area.
Restock long-term supplies and upgrade equipment.	Bulk office supplies, outdated equipment	Place bulk office supplies in priority-three area. Donate outdated equipment to local charity.
Review financial information, make adjustments for new year.	Computer printouts of annual profit/loss report, cash-flow analysis of previous year, budget and cash-flow projections for new year, marketing research for cash-flow projections, annual reports of client information	Computer is on desktop. Place long-term marketing research information in priority-two filing cabinet. Place previous year's taxes in storage box and take to priority-three area.
Conduct employee reviews. Store information for terminated employees.	Employee achievement reports, review sheets, paperwork for terminated employees	Place employee achievement reports in priority-two filing cabinet in office. Place records for terminated employees in priority-three area.
Review business plan and mission statement. Create new objectives.	Printouts of current business plan and mission statement, list of objectives	Place new mission statement in frame on wall. Replace old objectives list with a current list. Place a printout of your new business plan in your current files.

Applying the wisdom of the I Ching

Although a bit difficult to digest, the I Ching is a valuable guide for exploring the interaction between your work environment and your self-expression. An ancient text from which much feng shui wisdom originated, the I Ching can become a wise and helpful business associate. By examining how each of the "life situations" depicted in this text are represented in your work environment, you will be able to create a space that honors your life path and supports your deepest dreams and desires.

Water—
beginning the journey
Mountain—
finding inner strength
Thunder—
the strength of others
Wind—
tapping the source
Fire—
experiencing your success
Earth—
building trust
Lake—
response to fullness
Heaven—
the power of refinement

Water— beginning the journey

The Water trigram begins a journey into the unknown. Often translated as "New Beginnings" and "Chaos," this trigram represents setting a new course. This is the place at which each of us wonders, "What am I do to with my life?"

Answering this question requires a certain energy pattern, what noted psychologist Carl Jung referred to as the "hero archetype." Associated with the myth of the search for the Holy Grail—the one thing that will bring meaning to everything else—the hero finds himself at a crossroads, wondering how to direct his life energy. When you are at this point, you sense that everything else in your life goes on hold until you make this decision. To remain too long at this junction places you in a state of limbo and uncertainty, which can leave you feeling drained and apathetic.

To move through this stage, you must complete two tasks:

- You must first seek out your course, opening your heart and mind to numerous possibilities.

- You must make the decision (the commitment) to follow that course.

The Water trigram is associated with seeking out and committing to your life path. A life path is as essential to humans as water is to fish. Indeed, it is the water we swim in as we complete our individual journeys.

When you find yourself in a state of confusion, not sure of your life path, consider placing a "new beginnings" symbol, such as this glass egg, in the Journey trigram of your office. Eggs represent the cosmic soup, the chrysalis stage, in which a prior identity dissolves and provides the energy needed to birth a new form.

The journey gua

The Water trigram is controlled by the Journey gua, sometimes referred to as the Career gua. This area is always the front-center part of your home or office space. It is ruled by the element of Water, which is represented by organic flowing shapes, and downward moving energy. This energy pattern characterizes the soul's descent into the abyss. Unlike our modern approach, which fears the dark side of the psyche (the shadow aspects), the I Ching considers this descent a natural part of life's order. Only after a period of deep introspection and connection with "the ocean" of universal energy, can the hero emerge armed with his life's purpose.

It is this connection with the cosmic order that brings flow and peace to such a tumultuous time.

Flowing lines and natural organic shapes, such as this line of curvy desks, activate the energy of the Water trigram.

To represent your intention to connect with the cosmic order, consider placing any of the following in the front-center section of your desk or office:

- turtles (a symbol of creation and alignment with cosmic forces),

- a Quan Yin statue (the female goddess of peace and compassion), representing a willingness to participate in the human condition,

- the color black or dark blue,

- natural organic shapes with flowing lines,

- terraced or cascading arrangements,

- glass, mirrors, or other reflective surfaces,

- pictures of the ocean or a large body of water (avoid pictures of waterfalls),

- altars,

- hanging plants,

- flowing curtains,

- a vase with water and a single flower,

- a small fountain (avoid too much yang movement here).

Finding the right career

It is vital to your happiness and well being that you align yourself with the right business or career. You will know it is the right business for you if it provides opportunities to share yourself with others and grow into your vision of who you know yourself to be. Nothing is more frustrating than to know that you are not yet aligned with your "right" path and yet to feel blocked and unable to discern what that path is. Although many books have been written on this subject, your office can assist you in gaining clarity on this issue.

The black furniture and blue-tinted windows introduce Water energy into an otherwise Earth-energy brick building. The black recliner is especially appropriate. Any piece of furniture that gets your feet up off the ground helps you break ties with the walking persona of your daily life and merge with a larger consciousness. The more frequent the mergers, the clearer your path.

Have your windows cleaned. Windows represent vision and your ability to see your place in the world. A thin film of dirt can darken your entire outlook and depress you.

Remove any boxes, stacks of paper, or books from this area. This is not a place where you want the grounding influence of heavy items. Clutter or unsorted, unorganized items in this area are a physical manifestation of inner disjunction. By bringing order to the items in this area, you will restore mental clarity as well.

Place something in your window that catches the light. If you have lingered in a place of indecision for too long, you need to generate more yang chi in the area. Drawing light into the space shifts the yin/yang balance and helps to break up habitual ways of thinking.

Use a journal. Try "stream of consciousness" style journaling, where you start writing and do not stop until you have filled three pages. Do this every day for 27 days, focusing your intent on your desire to gain clarity. The first page tends to contain all the thoughts you rehearse over and again your mind. The following two pages help you move past that facade and access deeper levels of consciousness.

A journal can be a valuable tool for getting busy brains to relax enough to allow new insights and understandings to glimmer through. When journaling, be alert for those thoughts and ideas that seem to come from nowhere. Once you capture them in your journal, it is easier to find ways to manifest them in your life.

Perform the sun/moon mirror ritual. This is a Black Hat Tibetan Buddhist (BTB) ritual. Acquire two three-inch round mirrors. Place one in full sunlight for 27 days, taking it in and wrapping it in a silk cloth at night. Place the other mirror outside throughout the night, taking it in and wrapping it in a similar cloth in the morning. After the 27 days, glue the mirrors together, reflective sides out. This stage of the ritual symbolizes bringing the left and right sides of your brain together, creating clarity. Place the mirrors under your bed, directly under your head. Voice your willingness to accept your purpose (a very important and often difficult step) and ask for clarity in knowing what that purpose is.

The sun/moon mirror ritual is based on the feng shui precept that anything placed within your energy field while sleeping will have a greater impact on you than if you were awake. The filters we have up during the day relax once we move into the dream realm of the subconscious. Pay careful attention to what objects are in your energy field (usually it is whatever is under your bed) while you are asleep.

Create a collage. Collages use images and jumbled words to confuse the conscious mind and allow the subconscious room for expression. Include in your collage all the things that you love about you. Hang your collage in the Abundance area of your office. Whenever you look at it, ask yourself and the universe for insight in knowing what type of career would allow you to share those parts of yourself.

57

Your bulletin board makes an ideal backdrop for your on-going collage efforts. This collage was created from magazine clippings, client cards, inspirational thoughts, and favorite color swatches.

Handling resistance

Most of us desire to find our purpose because we want our lives to have meaning. The I Ching states that if "you can harmonize your aims and desires to the needs and flow of the cosmos, significant deeds will become possible." Finding and fulfilling a sense of purpose is the key to a meaningful life. The sun/moon mirror ritual described on page 57 cautions you against resisting your place in the cosmos. Noticing and letting go of your resistance is vital to move through the Journey trigram.

Noticing resistance. The best way to notice where your resistance lies is to take note of what is not happening in your life. Is there something you have been desiring for a long time that has not come to fruition? That is a great place to look for resistance. You can also identify where your resistance shows up in your environment and use the ba gua to help you discern exactly what that resistance is. Use the Ba Gua Map below to identify how you may have used your space to communicate your unconscious resistance to your conscious self.

Ba gua map

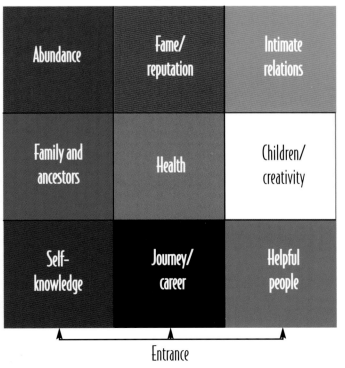

Abundance	Fame/ reputation	Intimate relations
Family and ancestors	Health	Children/ creativity
Self- knowledge	Journey/ career	Helpful people

Entrance

Look through your office space for any of the following blocks. These items or conditions indicate resistance on some level of your psyche.

- ☐ Boxes or paper piles that need to be sorted and put away
- ☐ An overflowing trash can
- ☐ Stagnant water
- ☐ Stagnant scents
- ☐ Stuck windows that should open but cannot
- ☐ Items blocking a door or covering up part of a window
- ☐ Pieces of furniture with broken or loose legs

Moving through resistance. Once you know what the physical manifestation of your resistance is, use that item or area to eliminate and remove that resistance.

- ☐ Sort through your papers and elevate any boxes off the floor.
- ☐ Buy a larger trash can or empty it more frequently.
- ☐ Eliminate stagnant water sources.
- ☐ Mist with distilled water and essential oils and open windows to clear out stagnant scents.
- ☐ Have a carpenter help you free any stuck windows.
- ☐ Reposition items so that they are not blocking a door or covering up part of a window.
- ☐ Repair any furniture pieces with broken or loose legs.

Making decisions

Once you have identified your life course, you still need to commit yourself to following it. Refusing to make this decision will impair your decision-making ability in general and leave you feeling uncertain about all types of choices.

What is your deciding process?

We all use different criteria to make our decisions. To know which of the following describes you, think about what you typically do when you buy a new car or new clothes.

Use your emotions as your guide. If you are excited about something, you buy it. If it makes you feel happy, beautiful, rich, or stylish, you buy it. You do not logically process the transaction or consider pros and cons, you go with your feelings.

Let your intuition guide you. Your gut tells you, "This is it," and you do not question. You might consider a few other options, but you do not really take them seriously because you have already "sensed" which option is best for you.

Use your experience as your guide. This is what we call personal knowledge—it includes everything you have experienced and learned in the past. When deciding on which item would be best, you process experiences you have had in the past, consider how it worked out for you, and decide on the item based on how you think it will perform for you in the future. This process also includes awareness of how your present situation might be similar or different from those of the past.

How you shop for clothes can provide valuable insight into your overall decision-making process. If you let emotions sway you while clothes shopping, chances are emotions will play a key role in your business decisions as well.

Use the knowledge or opinions of someone else to make your decision. You might read consumer reports because they have more knowledge about cars than you do. You might look at fashion magazines or follow the trends in your favorite store because they are "in the know." You might acquire what your neighbor has because they know more about a specific thing than you do. These approaches all rely on the expertise and knowledge of an outside source.

Apply a rational process to your decision. Here you apply a logical framework to the decision. The framework is external, but it is not based on another source. For example, you might take a used car to a garage and have them test it for various possible malfunctions. You use some form of logical reasoning or scientific method (hypothesis, experiment, measure findings, conclusions).

Getting to know the strengths and weaknesses of your decision-making process can provide a degree of self-awareness that will serve you both on and off the job.

How your decision-making pattern affects your work

To be successful in your business or chosen career, you need to understand the strengths and weaknesses of your primary decision-making pattern. If, for example, you use emotion as your guide, then days that are emotionally trying for you will not be days on which you will make wise business choices. If you rely heavily on the wisdom and knowledge of others and are unable to trust your own judgment, your uncertainty and need for external reinforcement can cripple you on those days when external reinforcement is not available (e.g., the bank tells you no, or your best client drops your service). Once you determine what your primary decision-making approach is, you can use the to Decision Making Approaches Chart on page 61 to find a way to balance that approach.

Decision-making approaches chart

	Strengths	Weaknesses
Personal emotions	Communicate the body's wisdom (rate of change is too fast, person is untrustworthy, etc.) Immediately available Apply to everything Forceful	Can be created by social norms or mental thought patterns that are not in your best interest Difficult to control, which makes them unreliable
Personal intuition	Provides connection to a source greater than the self (soul, spirit, divine influence, etc.) Immediately available Provides assistance with the unknown Independent of social norms Unlimited source of creativity and individualistic thinking	Difficult to discern, can lead to self-doubt and indecision Difficult to convince others of the viability or authenticity of these decisions
Personal experience	Creates reliability and constancy in your experience as all data is evaluated according to the same experiences Makes decisions based on personal criteria and hierarchies of importance	Uses the past to determine the future, subject to the limiting beliefs and understandings of the past Does not always contain all the information necessary to make the best decision
External influence	Allows you to use the expertise of others when your own is limited (specialization) Provides insight from a neutral, un-biased third party Allows you to understand alternative viewpoints	Is dependent upon the goodwill, knowledge, and motivations of other people; this method fails when those motivations and knowledge fail
Rational process	Produces verifiable, predictable results Provides a means by which to analyze the unknown Independent of personal emotions, which may not be reliable in a given situation	Ignores the heart and typically finds only that which it expects to find Discourages thinking "outside the box"

Combining decision-making approaches. Once you understand your primary approach to decision making, you are in a better position to balance that approach. We all need an internal and external decision-making standard, or we find ourselves unable to make crucial decisions.

Which approach could you add to your primary approach to bring more balance into your life? Applying the information from the Decision-making Approaches Chart on page 61 can help determine this.

How would your behavior change if you incorporated this decision-making strategy into your pattern? You might listen more to your instincts. You could read up on the latest discoveries. You may ask more people for their opinions. You might put processes in place to help you measure results.

Attention to internal and external sources, as well as rational and nonrational frameworks, can be combined to create a powerful decision-making process that draws on the strengths of each method while avoiding the weaknesses.

Delayed decisions

Not making a decision can be every bit as harmful as making the wrong one. Just as our reasons for making decisions vary, so, too, do our reasons for hesitating. Which of the following represents your primary reason for not making decisions?

- You find no joy in actually finishing the buying process. The joy comes in thinking about it, dreaming about how it will change your life, and considering options.

- You are not sure it is "perfect." You sense a gap between the fantasy life you want the object to provide and the actuality. Not deciding helps you avoid this awareness.

- You enjoy the attention of salespeople as you deliberate. To decide is to no longer have their attention.

- You do not believe you are worthy of having the object.

- You feel the need for more information and are unable to find ways of getting the information you need.

Know that, regardless of why you delay decisions, delayed decisions tie up your energy. If you delay for too long, your indecision will drain you of the very energy you need to make good decisions. This can result in a downward spiral that leaves you feeling more drained. If you are at this point, any decision will be helpful to you, because it will break this downward spiral. Take action and do not allow yourself to get bogged down with whether or not it is the right choice for you. Usually people find that in acting on a decision (even if they later find it was the wrong decision), they receive the insight they were waiting for. They can then change their course and move forward with their lives.

For most of us, delayed decisions at work mean a pile of papers, lunch refuse from the previous three days, and a hundred opened but unanswered e-mails. The more you postpone decisions, the more your energy is tied up in those issues and the less energy you have available to live your present moment. Gather all the information you need to make a good decision, but do not delay.

Mountain–
finding inner strength

As the brilliant moon begins to diminish just when it reaches fullness, and winter's coming becomes apparent even in summer, so, too, inferior and even hostile forces will interject themselves into the most perfect of careers. Like winter, these forces are in accordance with the patterns required to create inner strength. Only through adverse external conditions does inner strength develop.

 KEN

The mountain is the symbol of strength, solidarity, and self-reliance. This home office introduced a mountain motif through an etched-glass door.

If you cannot include an entire mountain, just a rock will do. This chunk of mountain was hewn from a local quarry and links the business with the strength of the entire neighboring mountain range.

The self-knowledge gua

The Mountain trigram is associated in the ba gua cycle with the Self-knowledge gua. The Self-knowledge gua is an Earth energy, dedicated to stillness, firmness, self-control, and self-mastery. This is a time of coming to know and overcome the forces of ego. To understand what motivates you and whether an action derives from an attempt to realign with the *Tao* (a name for the cosmic forces governing all life forms) or to satisfy the ego is the ultimate challenge of this gua. To know the difference between Tao and ego, and to have the internal control to silence the ego, is considered true wisdom.

The Self-knowledge gua is located in the front-left section of your office space.

This area should include:

- a picture of a mountain—the ultimate symbol of internal resources and stillness;

- books and journals, indicating the pursuit of wisdom;

- the means or tools of your daily practice, indicating self-control;

- large heavy Earth objects to ground/ stabilize the space;

- muted or grayed tones, adding Earth energy;

- rocks or stones, representing stillness;

- a paperweight on the front-left corner of your desktop;

- pictures of monks, athletes, or someone known for dedication and persistence;

- closed containers;

- a collage of self-exploration;

- a photograph of yourself.

There are many ways to set your intention for the day. Select a medium that speaks to you and will help you commit to a daily practice. Setting your intention can be as simple as drawing a card from a meditation card pack and taking a moment to reflect on the card's symbolism, simultaneously quieting your mind and creating space for your subconscious to speak to you.

Tracing your fingertips along the lines of this rock labyrinth opens channels to inner realms and is especially appropriate for the Self-knowledge area of a desk or office.

Daily practices

Internal reinforcements are drawn from the well of self-sufficiency and self-control. This internal well deepens and fills through daily actions. Consciously selecting your daily practices is a powerful way to know and master the self.

Recommended practices for increasing self-knowledge and mastery in a business setting include:

- clearing your desk. Try clearing your desk before you go home each day. It is a powerful way to put an end to your work day so that work does not mentally invade your after-work life. It also makes it much more enjoyable to start work the next day.

- setting your intention for the day. If you can, light a candle to give yourself a moment's pause dedicated to setting your intention for that day. If you cannot light candles where you work, consider setting your intention while you mist your office space with distilled water and essential oils.

- reviewing the day. A quick review of the day planner can become a ritual for processing what went well and what did not during the day. Asking to understand the larger pattern behind any upsets invites universal forces to be a part of your self-discovery process.

- taking a lunch break. To actually stop working while you eat your lunch honors your body and helps place whatever work you are doing into perspective.

- a gratitude call/note. Call or send a handwritten note to a favorite client, thanking them for their patronage. This daily practice will continuously remind you of your interdependent relationship with your clients and places your attention on what has gone well, instead of on what did not happen.

- getting outside. Leave your building, breathe fresh air, and see the sun at least once during the day. This practice will go a long way toward keeping you in balance. Our internal cycles (and emotions) can get out of sync if we do not see the sun for a couple of days.

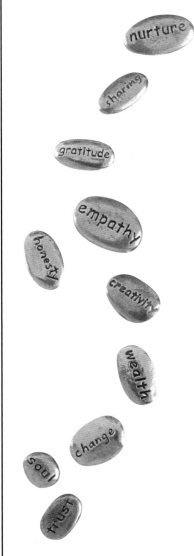

Words have mental and emotional impact. Surround yourself with words that reinforce internally the emotional and mental states you desire to experience.

Containers

Part of being the Mountain is to keep your energy self-contained. Mountains collect strength and draw other forces to them, rather than running frantically to and fro trying to gather resources. To collect and contain great reserves, you must have great containers. This section provides ideas for how to "containerize" your office to create optimal conditions for gathering resources.

Personalized containers. Take the time to find containers that speak to you personally—that match your style and your personality. You will have a lot more fun putting things away into those containers. One of the best tricks for getting yourself organized is to buy containers that you like so much, they draw your attention and constantly remind you to put things in order.

This consultant selected a spring green color for her client files. Spring green is a Wood-energy color and generates new business growth.

This container system allows this editor to continue adding more containers as her needs grow. Not one to settle for standard machine labels, she created her own labeling system by tying identification cards onto the handles.

Clear vertical stackers, such as those shown here, allow you to see the contents of the container. They are especially helpful for people who need visual reminders.

This vertical-stacking system sits right on your desktop and provides a way to keep your most active client files directly in front of you without stacking them in a pile.

Vertical vs. horizontal containers. If you tend to get lost in your piles of paper, it is probably because you have stacked those papers in a horizontal pile. Horizontal piles represent Earth energy. As a result, they feel dense, impenetrable, and heavy. Sort that same pile into a vertical-stacking file. You will be amazed at how easy it is to maneuver through your stack.

Closed vs. open containers. Closed containers are best for holding on to energy and allowing your strength to build. Open containers are better suited for the gathering/collecting stage.

Adequate amounts of containers. If you become overwhelmed easily, buy more containers. The more you break things down into smaller components, the easier they will be to deal with. Think for a moment about how difficult it would be find a file if you opened your file drawer and all the files were together in one large folder. Sorting those files into separate, smaller folders greatly facilitates filing as well as retrieving.

Sort before you contain. You will not know how many containers you will need, or what shape or size they should be, until you know what you have to place in them. Therefore, before you go out and buy your containers, you must pull everything out of that closet (or drawer, or filing cabinet) and sort it into piles in front of you. Once it is in piles, you will be able to make a quick list of how many containers you need, how big they must be, and what shape would work best. Then take that list when you go shopping. It will not do you any good to buy fun personalized containers if they do not fit your stuff.

Buy a labeler. Making clean crisp labels for your files cuts down retreival time, since the larger labels are easier to read.

After intentionally placing a photograph of a mountain behind his head, this client was able to break a long-term work relationship that was no longer healthy for him, and to launch his own company.

The wall behind the client's head was blank, offering him no internal reinforcement of his work identity.

What is behind your head

Because the Mountain trigram is concerned with identity and self-mastery, what you place on the wall behind your head is highly significant. To the Chinese, the space behind your head indicates what you think of yourself and how you choose to support yourself. A picture of a mountain, representing inner stillness and control over the ego is ideal.

Other "behind the head" themes include:

- architectural drawings, representing the foundation upon which something is built;

- art with squares or rectangles, representing a solid foundation;

- a rock garden or Zen garden, representing solidity, stillness, and inner peace;

- a person meditating or a scene that evokes a meditative state;

- books (if this is an actual bookshelf, make certain the books do not tower high above your head or project out at you, creating poison arrows);

- horizontal credenza that looks and feels solid.

Thunder– strength and support

CHEN

The Thunder trigram is rooted in the belief that life is sustained through self-perpetuating systems such as the food chain and the exchange of oxygen, nitrogen, and carbon dioxide among plants, animals, and the earth. For a business, it is the quality and quantity of your exchange with other systems that determines whether or not your business will thrive. Just as the nourishing rain follows the thunder, correct actions and choices on your part will nourish and grow your business.

The Thunder trigram emphasizes that our actions take place in an interconnected energy field, and that every work decision, not only affects our coworkers and other companies, but the larger living system that supports us all, the Earth.

The family and ancestors gua

Symbolically represented by the trunk of a growing tree, the Thunder trigram is situated in the Family and Ancestors area (middle left-hand section) of the ba gua. This placement indicates that we must learn to see ourselves (and our businesses) as part of a larger life cycle. To acknowledge and honor all that has gone before us, as well as all that will come after us, will bring the support of the universe and ensure greater success. No stream flows of its own accord and no grass grows without the sun and rain. Look around the Family and Ancestors area of your business. How do the items and overall decor represent your connection with all other life forms? Does this area feel supportive and strong? When you work in this space, are you receptive of the goodwill and support others are trying to offer you?

The trunk of the tree supports the branches, where the flowering and production of foliage and fruit occurs. Without the supportive trunk, there would be no flowering, no production, no leaves, and no fruit.

If you feel cut off from the natural world, consider replacing your laminate or metal cabinet with a wood one. This recycled teak cabinet adds texture, age, and vertical lift, as well as tucking files and supplies out of view.

To feng shui the Thunder trigram, consider the ways in which you would like to support and receive support from all other life forms. You might want to include some of the following:

- Healthy plant life (plants and humans are involved in a mutually symbiotic dance, constantly exchanging oxygen and carbon dioxide to support the other's continued life)

- Photographs of family members and friends

- Wood furniture (represents growth and strength)

- Tall vertical objects such as pillars, lamps, or columns

- Strong sturdy desks, no wobbly furniture

- Sound energy (stereos, radios, intercom system, bells or chimes: not shown)

When is it okay to bring your family to work? I worked with the owner of an interior design firm who forbid all his employees to have photographs of family, personal items, or plants on their desks. The overall effect was a beautiful, yet sterile environment. I recommended that he test his policy to see if it was actually in the best interests of his company. I asked that he permit each employee one family photograph, one plant, and one additional personal item of their choice for six months. At the end of the six months, his employee absentee rate had dropped by 28 percent and his turnover rate (which had been extremely high) had dropped by 62 percent. He decided to keep the new policy in place and continued to enjoy lower absentee and turnover rates.

Personal items and photographs encourage employee loyalty and increase employee longevity.

Too much family involvement, however, can also be problematic. Employees whose desks are cluttered with family photos and personal memorabilia have higher absentee rates. Whether it is because they take time off to care for children or to let a repairperson into the house, great employees suffer when the boundary between home and work is too weak.

Gather your team

You are not meant to do everything yourself. If you have a difficult time asking others for help, read that last sentence over again. All of life's cycles are inextricably linked to other cycles and work together to balance excess and harmonize discord. Are you trying to do too much by yourself? Could you work better if you took the time to build a team of supportive energies that worked in harmony with your energy?

The Thunder trigram cautions that to properly nourish yourself, according to the R. L. Wing translation of the I Ching, you must "be careful whom you give your nourishing energy to." In modern terms, this might read as, "be careful whom you support with your money." Hire people to help you (employees, subcontractors) and advisors to counsel you (accountants, lawyers, advertising firms) whose ethics and priorities are aligned with yours. If you "consistently nourish superior persons, who will in turn provide nourishment for others, you will achieve great effects." You cannot achieve superior results with an "inferior" team. An inferior team is one who indulges in negative or destructive thoughts, laziness, manipulation, or deceit. Identify and rout out any member of your support structure who engages in these destructive patterns.

Be certain to evaluate:

- employees,
- business partners,
- accountants,
- lawyers,
- public relations firms,
- advertising firms,
- business consultants or advisors,
- financial advisors and lenders.

Watch trends

Trends indicate where our society is at in the life cycle. For example, the 1980s was a decade of accumulation and excess. This period was followed by the Simplicity movement of the 1990s. Those who were watching this trend were prepared for the birth of the Simplicity movement and adjusted their business offerings to support it. As a result, they flourished as the movement flourished. This teaching contains a built-in caution, however. People who are too far ahead of their time will not meet with success when they advance their ideas and/or products. Good timing is vital to success. To improve your ability to interact with trends wisely, complete the following process.

The streamlined interior of this artist's studio exemplifies the Simplicity movement of the 1990s. This movement was a predictable swing given the excesses of the 1980s.

- Sketch out a life cycle for your industry. Think carefully about what stages that life cycle contains.

- Can you associate general trends with each of those stages? Be certain to consider trends in:
  - availability of free time,
  - amount and use of discretionary income,
  - relationship with nature,
  - connections with other human beings,
  - technological advances,
  - governmental and state regulations,
  - influence of foreign affairs,
  - eating behaviors,
  - physical fitness levels.

- Locate where you are presently in your industry's life cycle. Does this placement give you any information as to what you could expect in coming months or years?

- Consider whether your company's growth plans are in alignment with your industry's life cycle. Remember that to fight the cycle is to weaken and possibly destroy your business.

- Make any adjustments necessary to bring your business into harmony with your industry's cycle.

Time is another layer of interconnectedness to tune into. If your business depends on accurately forecasting trends, consider a clock as a symbol of how something that is constantly changing can support, rather than frustrate, you.

Form unlikely alliances

The Thunder trigram encourages us to pay attention to what is being nourished. In other words, where is your focus? Is it on mutual support and blessings, or is it on resentment, competition, and fear? Your attention is the key to transforming your business. More than your physical situation—cash flow, technological advantages, position in the industry—success comes to those who exercise unrelenting discipline over their thought patterns, and who cultivate only constructive opinions and attitudes in order to properly nourish the business. Consider how your business might change if you asked yourself the following question every time you interacted with a client, business associate, or competing business. Ask yourself, *"How can we mutually support each other through our efforts?"*

Instead of resenting clients for not giving you more work, or viewing other businesses as a potential threat, the Thunder trigram suggests that you look carefully for ways in which you could aid or support that client or business, and ways in which they could do the same for you. The more you see others as competition, the harder you will have to look. The shift will happen in your focus, not in their behavior.

For business associates who are not direct competitors, focus on areas of common interest. This opens a channel through which many things can flow, including information, projects, and a web of resulting relationships.

The interaction between your business and competing businesses can be a dance, rather than a struggle. Try viewing competing businesses as distant partners, there to serve the clients who don't fit your company's offerings.

You nourish that to which you give your attention and energy.

This is especially applicable for clients. To look for ways in which clients have blessed and supported your business is the seed of genuine gratitude. When you focus your attention on how your clients support you, your efforts to thank them feel genuine. As a result, you feel successful and they feel appreciated.

Many business owners know that they need to make this shift, yet find themselves trapped in destructive mental patterns. Begin by asking yourself where you have placed your focus. What types of things do you tend to notice? If you find that you are noticing what others have that you do not—opportunities, money, connections, power—or ways in which they have let you down, you stand to gain considerably by making this mental shift. Then support your intention to focus on mutually supportive relationships by making a few feng shui shifts in your office.

Your bulletin board can become a powerful ally in learning to control and direct your thoughts. Place items, photographs, clippings, notes, or anything else on your bulletin board that directs your thoughts toward the constructive opinions and attitudes you want to nourish.

Craft your business mantra. A mantra is a collection of sounds (we will use words) that hold a certain vibration and affect your mind in a consistent way. Many cultures use mantras to divert the mind from a deeply rutted thought pattern by replacing that pattern with sounds that generate an alternate pattern. Sound is a powerful assistant in altering mental patterns. The traditional Buddhist mantra for controlling thoughts is "Om Mah Ne Pad May Uhm" (phonetic spelling) The literal meaning is "The jewel is in the eye of the lotus." However, it is often translated as "I am one with the universe." If this mantra does not speak to you, try devising your own personalized phrase (sometimes called an affirmation), such as those listed below.

- I am open to receive blessings.
- When I honor my associates, I honor myself.
- I choose to give and receive assistance.
- I believe in synchronicity. All things are working together for my highest good.

The power of mantras and affirmations is in repetition. Your brain will often cycle through a destructive thought pattern repeatedly throughout the day. To counter such a strong force, write down your mantra and display it in the office. Train yourself to repeat it in your mind every time you happen to see it.

The literal translation of the Buddhist mantra Om Mah Ne Pad May Uhm is "The jewel is in the eye of the lotus." In Buddhist symbology, the lotus represents one's opening into transcendence.

Bring music into the office. Just as a combination of words can alter your thought patterns, so can music. Music without words can be especially helpful here. Because it uses sounds instead of words to generate a vibration, you can benefit from music in those times when you do not have the words to describe what you need. It is especially difficult for right-brained people to come up with words to describe a feeling state.

- Experiment with different types of music, noting their effect on both your body and mind.

- Select CDs or songs that create strong emotional effects.

- Play those CDs or songs every time you need the assistance of those emotions.

- The more you repeat (just as with the mantras), the more powerful the effect.

It takes a lot of energy to hold a vibration in place. Adding a stereo to your office makes it easier for you to sustain the right kind of mood throughout your work day.

If mantras are not for you, you can still harness the healing power of sound by tuning in to your music. Invest in a CD collection that both inspires and calms you and familiarize yourself with the emotional and energetic effect each CD has on you. Then you will know what you need to listen to on any given day.

Predecessor energy

The Family and Ancestors area of your business is strongly linked to predecessor energies. All that has happened before you is energetically held in this area of your business. If you have located your business in a building where the previous business experienced problems, you will want to perform a space-clearing for this area. The right type of space-clearing can remove the debilitating patterns of the previous business from the energy field of the building. To leave such patterns in place is to invite those patterns to take hold in your business.

Space-clearing with language and intention. A powerful form of space-clearing is to couple language with intention. This form of clearing requires no ritualistic objects such as candles, bells, or incense. Instead, it uses the power of words and visualization to transmute energy fields. The Space-clearing Steps Chart below is a variation of a Perelandra process that Machealle Small Wright describes in her *Garden Workbook II*.

Although you do not need any ritual objects to help you complete this process, feel free to light candles or mist the area with distilled water to aid you in altering your consciousness for this process.

Space-clearing steps chart

1	Identify the area to be cleared. This would be the Family and Ancestors area (middle left-hand section) of the entire building. If you only have a portion of the building, clear the Family and Ancestors area of your office.
2	Take a photograph or draw a floor plan of the area to be cleared. This will aid you in your visualization.
3	If possible, seat yourself in the area you are clearing.
4	Place the diagram or photo in front of you so that you can see it.
5	State your intention to the space, using the following language: "I am here to clear this space of any energies that are not in harmony with the intent or success of _____." (Fill in the blank with the name of your business.)

6 Imagine a beam of white light over your head. See the rays from this light move down over you and envelop you in white light. State: "I ask that this light assist me, so that what I am about to do is in harmony with my highest good. I ask that this light help me transmute the ungrounded emotional energies released by us humans and that I be fully protected during this process. I welcome your presence and thank you for your help."

7 Imagine a beam of green light over your head. See the rays from this beam envelop you, commingling with the white light. State: "I ask that the light of nature aid me in releasing and collecting the energies absorbed by the nature kingdoms, tangible and intangible, animate and inanimate. I also ask that the light of nature aid me so that what I am about to do is for the highest good of the planet Earth. I welcome your presence and thank you for your help."

8 Focusing on the drawing or photo, state, "I ask that any energies that are ungrounded, stagnant, inappropriate, or out of harmony with my intention be released from this area. I request this in gentleness and love, knowing that the cleansing and transmutation process I am about to be a part of is a process of life enhancement, and not negation."

9 Visualize the area to be cleared. Visualize a white sheet of light forming five feet below the area. Allow the edges of the sheet to extend five feet beyond the boundary of the area. Ask that the white light and the light of nature join you as together you lift the white sheet up through the area to be cleansed. Allow the sheet to rise five feet above the highest point.

10 Carefully gather the corners of the sheet in your mind's eye, and using visualization, form a bundle that encloses all the released energies contained in the sheet. To the left of the bundle, see a gold thread. Tie the bundle closed with this thread. To the right of the bundle, see another gold thread. Tie the bundle with that thread as well.

11 State: "I now release the bundle to the white light and to the light of nature so that the energies that have been released from this area can be moved on to their next highest level for transmutations and the continuation of their own evolutionary processes."

12 Focus again in your mind's eye on the area you just cleared. Notice any differences. Thank the forces that aided you and ask to be disconnected from those forces.

You have completed the space-clearing process. You can now expect to feel clean, unlimited, and insightful in the space that you cleared.

Wind–
tapping the source

A deeply satisfying business is one that reflects your true essence and allows you to share that essence with others. If you share truly of yourself, you are in harmony with the cosmic order. In the I Ching, cosmic order is the force that brings the development of human beings and the needs of the universe into symbiotic harmony. "When the individual and the cosmos are in harmony, human potential is enhanced and many things flourish."

The amazing power of the Wind trigram has been described in American psychology as "synchronicity." Synchronicity is psychologist Carl Jung's term for positive actions that trigger a seemingly unrelated string of beneficial events. Jung believed that it was impossible to send a high vibration (such as peace, hope, and trust) out into the world without it resonating with and activating similar vibrations in other life forms. He believed that these life forms respond to that vibration by sending back a corresponding vibration, which shows up in the person's life as happy helpful synchronicities.

The Wind trigram is a constant flow of the opportunities, assistance, and other forms of synchronicity that provide opportunities and growth for both individuals and businesses. Learning how to activate and control the energy of Wind is a significant challenge for any business.

HSUN

Wind chimes have been used for centuries as wealth guardians and as symbols of opportunity. Even an indoor wind chime carries this symbolism.

The abundance gua

The Wind trigram is controlled by the Abundance gua. Located in the rear-left corner of your office or building, this gua governs your relationship to money. The yin base line followed by two yang lines makes this a gua of power and driving energy. Like the wind—the force that turns windmills—this energy pattern is concerned with generating industry and achievement.

As you might imagine, feng shui symbols for activating this gua are many, including:

- tall vertical objects (representing growth);
- bamboo (its fast growth represents speedy aid and its flexible branches connote that sometimes it is necessary is to bend in the wind);
- sailing ships with full sails;
- a three-legged toad carrying a coin in his mouth;
- I Ching coins;
- hollow metal wind chimes;
- pictures of the sky, airplanes, kites, or anything else that moves through the air;
- mobiles;
- fish (especially goldfish or koi, as they were considered by the Chinese to bring financial fortune);
- fountains with a visible base.

The popular bamboo is a great way to bring strong Wind energy into your office. Bamboo is associated with wealth because it represents versatility (it could be made into anything), perseverance (it continually grows), and sustainability (its rapid growth means you can harvest the same plant every six years).

Hanging a kite in your office represents your ability to use the winds of change to your advantage, rather than ignoring or fearing change. This kite is also a mobile and pictures women dancing and charming the wind.

This spring green wall is literally the color of active leadership. To increase your ability to move people and projects forward toward eventual success, use yellow-green.

Penetrating leadership

Just as the wind can penetrate the densest brush, the energy of the Wind trigram finds a way to go where no one has gone before. This ability to see into the hidden future is what creates leaders in any industry. Often described as "visionaries," successful entrepreneurs are able to see what others cannot—the ways things could be. Because of the strength of this vision, the entrepreneur is able to gather around him helpful people who can assist him in transforming his dream into reality. However, the I Ching warns that "if the vision is faint or the vessel is weak, there will be misfortune." If the leader loses sight of his vision, or if he succumbs to other forces (such as greed) and loses his personal integrity, everyone involved in the business will suffer with him.

Becoming a strong leader. You can increase your natural leadership abilities by "penetrating to the Source of people's motivations." These sociobiological promptings are your key to discerning future events. Simply asking what you can do to serve a genuine human need will put you in touch with your own intuitive knowing. Each of us has what the I Ching calls "a natural adaptation." This gift is the ability to penetrate into the real need hiding behind a human issue and to discern, by the power of our experiences and abilities, the solution to that need. Our life's work then is to bring our vision of the solution into the physical world. To ignore the needs of those around us, or to ignore the insight of our own "natural adaptation," will bring misery and misfortune.

When dried, bamboo becomes even more versatile and helpful than living bamboo. Easterners use dried bamboo like Westerners use metal to cocreate with nature anything from a table to a chair to a house.

Increasing your Wood energy. For those with weak Wood energy, the process of envisioning a possible future is difficult. They see only what is in the "here and now." You can support your desire to envision possibilities by increasing the Wood energy in your office space. Wood is strong, active, vertical energy. Like a good leader, Wood energy is decisive and moves quickly, but it is also flexible and able to make changes when necessary. The following are especially potent ways to nurture Wood energy in your work space.

- Use a spring green color in your decor or business materials.

- Avoid muted tones or colors with a lot of gray in them (such as sage green or taupe).

- Include an outdoor or indoor fountain with water that shoots up in the center.

- Add growing, thriving plants, especially plants with strong vertical movement.

- Use live or dried bamboo (known for its strength, as well as its flexibility).

- Get regular exercise.

- Bring music into your work space.

- Arrange your desk so that you have an expansive view out of a window.

- Place a torchère lamp or hang a mobile in the rear-left corner of the room in the Abundance sector.

- Mist your space with a mister bottle of distilled water and essential oils.

To change your feelings about budgeting and finances, try changing the container. Instead of stuffing your bills or printed budgets into the back of a drawer, place them in a beautiful container, such as this spring green leather binder. The container can alter your mood, which can change your thinking.

This beautiful box made of bamboo was used to help a business owner transform the task of bill-paying into a ritual affirming her inherent Abundance.

Coming to terms with your finances

This section is especially for those of you who run your own business. Ignoring your finances is equivalent to sure death in the business world. Although you might be tempted to avoid looking at your finances because you know the situation is not a good one, ignorance and avoidance are antithetical to the Wind trigram's visionary leadership. To translate feng shui terms into the language of finance, Wind energy is the equivalent of cash flow. Cash pays bills, makes payroll, and finances expansion. Without adequate cash flow, potentially profitable businesses will fail. At the risk of sounding like a banker, the best feng shui cure you can do for your business is to review a 12-month cash flow analysis every month and make financial choices accordingly. A cash flow analysis gives you the means for controlling the wild nature of the Wind trigram, and increases your foresight as to how much money you need to come up with and when you need to have it. This knowledge makes you financially flexible and responsible. To put metaphysical feng shui cures in place while failing to perform a cash flow analysis is to misunderstand the nature of Wind. The Wind brings sudden growth and opportunities. However, sudden growth requires tremendous responsibility, strong management, and keen foresight or it will lead to disaster and bankruptcy.

Personal finances. If you do not own your own business, creating and living according to a budget will bring similar financial responsibility and control into your life. If you resist budgets, give some careful thought to how your resistance to control in general might be undermining your dreams. You can let go of that resistance by "owning" the activity, making it fit your personality and style. How about tracking your daily expenditures in a funky green notepad or a red leather day planner? If you are computer literate, try personalizing the formatting on your accounting-software reports or renaming traditional categories to better suit you. Maybe a palm pilot will make budgeting fun and practical enough that you can let go of your resistance. However you do it, get real with yourself about your money. The number one feng shui rule to remember when it comes to managing money is that avoidance is not good management.

Enhancing financial opportunities

Once you put systems in place to responsibly manage your finances, you are in a good position to tap into the flow of the wind.

Calling on the wind horse. The wind horse represents the nature of opportunity. Imagine that you are standing in the center of a field. You can hear a horse thundering up behind you. You have only one chance to grab the horse's mane, swing yourself up onto the saddle, and ride the horse. This is the nature of opportunity. To be able to take action in those moments when the universe presents you with an opportunity is one way to harness Wind. Those who delay or hesitate miss their chance, and the horse thunders on without them. To increase your ability to ride the Wind horse, place a small running horse in the rear-left corner of your desk.

Expanding your current resources. To represent your willingness to realize the potential for expansion in your current situation, use an object in your office in a unique and unusual way. For example, you might use an exercise ball for a chair, plant a fern in an old teapot, or hang an item upside down. As you think about how you could use an existing object in a novel way, ask the universe to help you understand how your existing resources could be used to create new and exciting opportunities for you.

Creating a money tree. One way to physically manifest your intention to increase abundance is to create a money tree. Place three I Ching coins underneath a jade plant and place the plant next to the cash register (if you have one) or in the rear-left corner of your desk. The three coins represent harmony between heaven's forces, earth's forces, and your own efforts to generate abundance in your life. The jade plant represents wealth, as its leaves are shaped like coins. By placing the coins under the plant, it metaphorically represents grafting the plants growth energy to your financial situation.

Horses run like the wind, representing opportunities and the financial ability to take advantage of those opportunities when they come galloping by.

These three I Ching coins represent harmony between the forces of heaven, earth, and man. Placing three coins next to lucky bamboo (or a jade plant) is a ritual for activating fast growth in the company's finances.

Horses are especially appropriate in the Hsun trigram. Before the horse was tamed, man was limited to how much distance he could cover in a day. After taming the horse, his ability to travel distances increased exponentially. To create exponential growth in your business, include horses.

Transplanting any plants that have overgrown their pots represents making room for growth in other areas of your business.

Increasing your tolerance of change

Another symbol of strong Wind energy is the ability to tolerate change. Change is an essential component of transforming something from a potential state into an actuality. Although many people dream of what they would like to do, only people with strong Wood energy know how to turn those dreams into reality. You can increase this ability within yourself by increasing your flexibility and comfort level with change.

Pull up your roots. Transplant any plants that have outgrown their pots. Overgrown plants represent resistance to change and the inability to put growth to good use. Make certain the new pot is large enough to support quite a bit of new growth. Add a small amount of fertilizer to the soil when you repot the plant, representing new energy and an increased ability on your part to handle the change.

Incorporate the infinity symbol in your artwork. The infinity symbol, drawn as a sideways eight, represents openness to the endless possibilities that exist in the universe, as well as the constant transfer of energy from one form into another. By bringing an infinity symbol into your office space, you affirm your intention to remain open to possibilities, regardless of how strange or far-fetched they may appear to be.

Move 27 items. There are numerous variations of this ritual. A great business variation is to move one item in your office every day for 27 days. As Spencer Johnson, the author of the best-selling book *Who Moved My Cheese?* points out, we all get rigid and a bit stuck in our ways of processing the world, doing things a certain way because that is the way we have always done it. This moving ritual can support your desire to lighten up and relax, as well as learn to actually enjoy change. Even though change can be disconcerting, just simply give yourself permission to make small changes in your office will make it easier to give yourself permission to make other changes.

Fire– experiencing your success

 LI

In the Li trigram, use fire shapes and symbols, such as an uplight torchère lamp, essential oils that activate the senses, and wall art that moves the eye up instead of down.

The Fire trigram is about opening to receive all the light, success, and admiration that flows naturally to you when you follow your life's calling. This trigram comes immediately after the Wind trigram in the life cycle. While Wind concerns itself more with an abundance of opportunities and the wealth that can come from those opportunities, Fire reigns over reputation and how you are perceived by clients, colleagues, and competing businesses alike. How comfortable you are receiving admiration and gratitude from others will determine how you experience the energy of this trigram.

The R. L. Wing translation of the I Ching refers to this time of great success and admiration as the Zenith. This stage is one of peak expansion, "as in the moment of the full moon, the longest day of the year, of the heights of personal esteem." This is a time when goals are realized, dreams have become reality, and you have given your all. This is also the time for others to notice what you have accomplished and the gifts you have shared. They desire the opportunity to admire and thank you for your sharing.

The fame gua

Associated with the transforming power of the mystical Phoenix, the Fame trigram is about knowing that our gifts and contributions have value and meaning in the world. Located in the rear center of your office, your Fame gua is where you get to shine your own light, recognize your accomplishments, and experience the thanks and gratitude of others. Governed by Fire energy, the Fame gua needs lots of light, activity, and sociability. Part of designing your Fame gua is to ask yourself what it is that you would like to be recognized for? How would someone show you that your efforts had made a meaningful difference? Examine the rear-center area of your office to see what messages you are sending the world regarding your personal value.

Enhancing your Fame energy can be as simple as hanging this "Shine" picture frame on your bulletin board. Held in place by charming magnets, this picture of self should be one that shows you at your best.

The bright colors in this collaged frame bring the energy of fire into the Fame gua. The sayings on the collage represent that for which this client would like to be known in the world.

Letting others know what you want

As children we communicated our needs for attention and feedback freely. My niece often twirls around like a ballerina, declaring "Look at me, aren't I a good dancer?" My son, however, lets me know that he wants to be recognized for his quick wit and ability to memorize movie lines. With so few people able to read minds, we need to communicate to the world how we want them to recognize and praise us. To tell my son what a great dancer he is would leave him feeling flat and frustrated. To ask my niece to relate lines from last night's movie would make her feel awkward and confused. Look around your office and ask yourself what message you are sending to clients and coworkers. Use the Recognition Chart on page 94 for ideas on how to communicate the right message.

This client meeting area is perfect for the Fame gua, including fire symbols such as animal skins in the couch, birds in the wall art, lots of natural light, and furniture placed to create a triangle.

Depending on what you find, you might want to enhance this area in any of the following ways.

- Use triangular and sunburst shapes to activate Fire energy.

- Give yourself an expansive view in this direction, even if it is by hanging a picture or a mirror on the wall.

- Raise blinds and bring as much natural light into this area as possible.

- Display items you are proud of that give you a sense of personal accomplishment.

- Include Fire-energy symbols as decor objects, such as candles or incense.

- Add a color spot to bring intensity and passion to this area.

- Display items from others that communicate their thanks and admiration.

- Remove heavy items from the floor and make this area as expansive as possible.

PHOTOGRAPHS

PHOTOGRAPHS

情熱

PASSION

Recognition chart

I would like to be recognized for	Possible feng shui adjustments
My sense of humor	Sunlight, laughter, cartoon art
My drive and initiative	Live bamboo stalks or a thriving green plant
My compassion and depth of feeling	Candles, an open office door
My ingenuity and creative solutions	Original artwork, novel use of common items
My ability to bring everyone together	Groupings of three or more, wreaths, circles
My precision and attention to detail	White trim, straight lines, geometric patterns
My sense of style	Unique combinations or groupings, strong use of color, personal wall art, personal items on desk
The depth of my knowledge	Books, journals, examples of personal contributions to the field, publications, stones and rocks
My eye for: color, a great deal, a worthy investment, a future product, profitable real estate, competent employees, etc.	Symbolic object of what you intuit; could be a throw rug with fun color combinations, framed coins, packaging ideas, pictures of real estate, reports of employee longevity
My problem-solving abilities	Puzzles, sample products, mazes, visually complex wall art (Escher, Dali, Picasso), metal items
My personal integrity and honor	Vase with water, black items or picture frames
My ability to lead a team	Green color, tall vertical objects, conference table
My delight in the present moment	Cut flowers, butterflies, music, pictures of birds, floral or citrus scents, hot tea
My social skills	Large office area, comfortable meeting chairs for clients
My computer skills in: design, programming, layout, word processing, etc.	Computer placed in rear center of desk or rear center of office
My gift of discovering incredible beauty in the ordinary	Fresh flowers (cut or potted), personalized touches, use of natural materials in desk selection and office design, color combinations involving more than two colors
My tendency to nurture and care for the needs of others	Pillows, pastels, terra-cotta pots, containers, food or drink service, meeting chairs
My honesty with self and others	Picture of ocean or large body of water, black and dark blue colors, reflective surfaces, mirrors, glass

Giving yourself permission

Allowing yourself to fully recognize your own accomplishments and to experience praise is not always easy. Many have been successful in the eyes of others without allowing themselves to experience their own success. Once you know what form of recognition you would like to experience, the next step is giving yourself permission to experience that recognition.

Permission requires opening and letting down boundaries between yourself and others. The following feng shui items and actions represent the dissolution of boundaries and a merger with other energy forms.

- Light a candle daily.
- Use butterflies, dragonflies, or birds in your decor scheme.
- Take the lid off closed containers.
- Sit next to your clients instead of across the desk from them.
- Let in as much natural light as possible.
- Eliminate black-and-white color schemes.
- Try a multicolored flower arrangement.
- Open your office door or windows more often.
- Create a place for others to sit in your office.

If all this focus on success and recognition feels selfish to you, remember that the I Ching considers success an opportunity to increase your understanding of self and your ability to help others. "Your motivations may begin to take on completely new directions. Just at the moment when you feel the greatest self-possession. Learning to understand this natural tendency in inner development is a true gift in understanding yourself and others. The Zenith of inner awareness is a fascinating time for self-discovery."

Skylights are ideal in Fame, but be certain to provide covering for times when the heat and exposure become too intense.

The vertical energy of this arrangement requires an open container. Try taking the lids off of your containers to increase yang movement in the business.

By creating a place for others to sit, you align your office with the social nature of the Fame gua.

96

Earth— building trust

The Earth trigram is represented by three broken lines, the triple yin symbol. This is a time and space for building long-lasting business relationships on a foundation of mutual trust. Trust is a pivotal issue in business relations.

Include photos in this area of people and animals that you love and trust. Eliminate any photos or references to untrustworthy people.

☰☰ KUN

There are three parts to this issue:

- You must become trustworthy yourself in all your business interactions.

- You must decide who is and is not trustworthy. This is a necessary part of developing your powers of discernment. Those who are not trustworthy should be avoided.

- You must learn to give your trust to others when appropriate.

The intimate relations gua

In the ba gua cycle, the Earth trigram is the symbol for the Intimate Relations gua. Because it is an Earth-energy sector, the Intimate Relations gua provides the support and nurturing energy for everything that follows in the ba gua cycle. Although the Intimate Relations gua is often associated with marriage, in a business, the issue of trust revolves around clients, business associates, and other businesses. A thriving business requires that you gain and extend trust.

Locate the Intimate Relations area of your office or work building. Does this area hold items that connote trust, longevity, and the ability to sustain relationships over time? Are there signs that untrustworthy people might be currently affecting you? If your trash can is located there, do you have people in your circle that you need to let go of, or is it that you tend to let people go too quickly because you are afraid of lasting relationships? A careful look at this area can help you know where you stand with regards to the trust issue.

Aligning your verbal message. Your web-site message, the text in your marketing brochure, the way you describe yourself and your business to others, and your company policies and procedures are all verbal messages by which you make your promise known to the world. Once you know what your promise is, you can set about making sure all your verbal messages are in harmony with that promise. Any time you identify a phrase or word that is in conflict or otherwise unsupportive of your promise, you must rout it out of your business.

Aligning your visual message. Just as important, if not more so, than your verbal message is your business's visual message. The eye supplies what the mouth does not or cannot say. Your visual message must be in alignment with both your verbal message and your overall business promise.

CommUnity Resolution, Inc., is an environmental consulting firm, specializing in mediation. Their logo:
• represents people coming together around environmental issues;
• uses a central symbol with numerous meanings—a leaf, a tree, a table around which people gather;
• uses an outer circle that surrounds and protects the inner circle, representing individuals and groups who protect the environment;
• incorporates the color green for the environment.

The three crucial areas to analyze for visual alignment are:

☐ the images, shapes, and colors you use in your marketing materials;

☐ the condition and look of your reception area;

☐ the appearance of your employees.

The Self Start logo uses a growing sapling to represent the company's focus on providing training and business coaching to "budding" business ventures.

WasherWomen, Inc., is a woman-owned business that collects laundry from ships docking in the Port of Houston and returns clean laundry before ships sail. Their logo:
• depicts distinctive name,
• promises old-fashioned hardworking service,
• uses a circle to denote a ship's porthole.

The Watering Can, Inc., is a florist shop with an interior landscaping business. Their logo:
• illustrates the distinctive business name,
• illustrates the product and services provided—plants and plant maintenance,
• implies sophistication through a bromeliad plant, which helps sell services to corporate clients.

Indications that a business is both trustworthy and trusting include:

- organic materials, such as ceramic pots for your plants or natural tile on your floor;

- oak or other hardwoods in flooring, counters, or desks;

- quality building materials that will last over time;

- containers of all sorts;

- potted plants;

- paperweights or other grounding objects;

- rocks, stones, gemstones, and unpolished crystals;

- permanent or built-in fixtures (not in photo).

Build
Your
Future

You earn the trust of others by refusing to pretend to be something you are not. When you let go of the pretense, you will find that it is possible to become your vision by daring to take the daily actions necessary to do so.

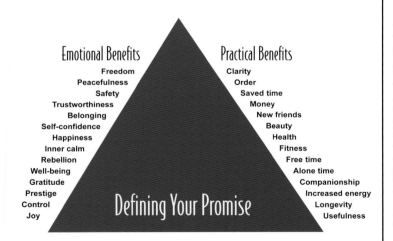

Emotional Benefits	Practical Benefits
Freedom	Clarity
Peacefulness	Order
Safety	Saved time
Trustworthiness	Money
Belonging	New friends
Self-confidence	Beauty
Happiness	Health
Inner calm	Fitness
Rebellion	Free time
Well-being	Alone time
Gratitude	Companionship
Prestige	Increased energy
Control	Longevity
Joy	Usefulness

Defining Your Promise

Every business promises its customers something. To understand your company's promise, identify the functional and emotional benefits of your product or service.

Deserve the trust of others

In the business world, customer loyalty is called "goodwill." Goodwill is your ability to draw the same customers and clients, time and again, because they have a bond with you or your product. Goodwill is a strong enough factor that it often affects the selling price of a business or a bank's decision to give you a loan. To increase goodwill in your business according to the I Ching, the Earth trigram counsels that "Sincerity inspires confidence." People respond to the real deal. No one appreciates being duped or manipulated. You must go out of your way to insure that nothing you do results in this experience for your clients. There are two primary areas to look at: your verbal message and your visual message. In your marketing, you must make certain that all your text, policies, and written promises (your verbal message) as well as your marketing materials, your reception area, and your company's dress code (your visual message) are all in alignment with your promise to the customer.

Defining your promise. Every company extends a promise to its customers and clients. This promise includes both functional and emotional benefits. Harley Davidson® promises its customers adult rebellion and Volvo® promises a safe ride. If you were to describe your company's promise in a single phrase, what would it be? One way to figure this out is to ask, "What human need is my service or product filling?"

Find the need, and you will discover your promise. This promise is what the marketing world calls a "brand," but it is much more than a logo or a tagline. Your promise is a part of every business decision you make.

Color symbolism for businesses

Color symbolism goes beyond good design. The meaning attached to color can make or break a business. For example, in new American industries, the first two colors most commonly branded are red and blue. Competitors using other colors in their marketing are seen as runners-up to the red company and the blue company. International markets require a much more diverse color analysis, as color symbolism shifts dramatically when it crosses national boundaries. Good feng shui means knowing what the colors you are using mean in the minds of your target market. The following information is the result of a three-year survey of 30,000-plus participants from over 30 countries (83 percent of respondents were Americans). The most common association is listed first. Companies strongly associated with a specific color have been included in parentheses.

Color	Symbolism
White	Purity, cleanliness, scientific approach, artificial quality, deity
Black	Sophistication, death and mourning, modernity, high quality, introversion
Gray	Intelligence and mental activity, decay and decline, duty
Gold	Monetary exchange, deity, expensive price tags, royalty, fake quality (American Express, Porsche)
Silver	Technological advancements, polished and smooth quality, computers including internet service
Brown	Reliability, common/inexpensive quality, strength, Mother Earth, frugality (UPS, PowerBar)
Red	Power, anger, passion, appetite, activity, sex appeal (3M, MasterCard, Coca-Cola, Costco, Verizon, Wells Fargo, Xerox, American Red Cross, Macintosh)
Orange	Ripeness, change, humor, activity, harvest (Home Depot, Southwest Airlines, Monster)
Yellow	Warmth, energy, friendliness, optimism, cheerfulness, social events (McDonalds, BestBuy, Kodak)
Green	Nature, health, good luck, environmentally friendly, greed (Fuji, Healthy Planet, Earthjustice)
Blue	Healing, peacefulness, dependable service, serenity (IBM, Wal-Mart, Delta, Intel, Altius)
Navy blue	Civil service, intelligence, depth, introspection
Purple	Attorneys and intellectual property, dignity, royalty, expensive items, flamboyance
Favorites	Blue, yellow, purple, green, red
Least favorites	Orange, muddy yellow, olive green, brown

Avoid those who are not trustworthy

The I Ching teaches that stagnation is brought about by interaction with inferior persons. A person is considered "inferior" when that person cannot be trusted. Later the text states: "There exists no advantage, even to persons of exceptional character and virtue, to engage in interactions with inferior persons." There will be people with whom you simply do not connect—you do not think the same way; you do not act the same way. When you try to interact with them, confusion and discord are the results. It is best to avoid interactions with such people and to withdraw yourself from situations that require those interactions.

Before her feng shui consultation, this therapist's chair was further to the left, where the edge of the wall creates a "poison arrow." The new placement removes the arrow from her back, putting her in a safer position, and also communication to her clients that she is able to provide them with the safety they need.

Items to adjust in your office to support your intention to avoid untrustworthy individuals include:

- sharp edges inside the office, such as filing cabinets, where the sharp edge is directed at your back while you are seated;
- sharp edges outside the office, directed at your back through a window;
- sitting in front of a window;
- sitting with your back to the door.

Cooperation requires trust

As important as it is to withhold your trust from untrustworthy persons, it is equally important to give your trust in order to form strong and lasting relationships with others. "Unity brings good fortune," are the I Ching's encouraging words. "The individual human spirit is nourished by a sense of connectedness to the whole of human awareness." To refuse to give your trust can cut you off from the very people who would support and strengthen you. In terms of business, lasting growth happens, not in a vacuum, but in cooperation with other human efforts.

Symbols of connection and trust are:

- anything circular (ring of community);
- business cards from supporting businesses;
- promotional efforts to reward your best customers;
- brick, stone, or other building materials made from earth;
- crystals and geodes.

Lake— response to fullness

No other trigram has more disparate names and associations than the Lake trigram. Referred to as "Joyous Lake," "Excess," "Fullness," "Openness," and "Decline," this trigram illustrates the many ways human beings respond to an experience of fullness. The same experience of fullness could be used to open one to a greater understanding and appreciation of the universe or to glut one's resources and behave excessively. The simplest way to understand how you respond to the energy of this trigram is to think about how you react when you find that you have more than enough money at the moment. When you have "disposable income," do you spend it or save it? If you tend to spend money, what types of pleasures do you spend it on? Thinking about your honest response to these questions will help you create a healthy relationship with the energy of the Lake trigram.

 TUI

When your physical space is overflowing with stuff, you communicate an inability to receive more from the universe. Make room for what you desire by clearing that which you no longer need.

Slow down your spending through purchasing potted flowers, rather than cut flowers. You can still enjoy the beauty of the flowers, without the weekly expense.

If shopping is your response to "fullness," increase Earth energy through muted colors or heavy grounded objects.

If you tend to spend

A common response to the experience of temporary fullness is to spend. Unaccustomed to fullness, it is tempting to give it all away just as soon as it comes in, unconsciously returning matters to their original state of scarcity or having "just enough." If you have this pattern in your personal life, it will carry over into your business. Unfortunately, this pattern spells death for cash flow, since every business has times of plenty when resources need to be stored for following periods of famine. To adjust for this pattern, using feng shui, find a way to express fullness with less. This does not mean that you decorate your office with a Zen minimal style, but you should look for areas that feel excessive or items that you tend to buy time and again, even though you do not need more.

- Paint your office. Use paint to add richness to a room instead of new furnishings.

- Take delight in small pleasures. Small pleasures can help you to feel rich without draining your pocketbook, such as a subscription to your favorite hobby magazine or a funky coffee mug.

- Reduce for elegance. Clear out a shelf of knick-knacks and position one or two favorite items in their place.

- Buy potted flowers. The fullness of potted blooms tends to last three times longer than cut flowers.

- Use spot color. Satiate your need for new by repainting a spot-color wall a different color every time the seasons change.

- Rotate. Store and rotate your decor items so that each fiscal quarter brings a new look, as well as a new budget.

- Tune in. You will find you feel satiated and need moments of excess less when you are fully present during the experience.

If you need to loosen up

The energetic opposite of the spendthrift is the person who cannot allow himself to enjoy or find pleasure in his situation. This person is afraid that to open up, relax, and let it all go is to lose everything he has worked so hard to attain. The feng shui adjustments to help shift this dynamic are quite different from those recommended for spenders.

- Wise investments. Invest in capital expenditures that will make your life easier over the long run.

- Update old equipment. It is often easier to spend money on items that will increase your productivity.

- Personal touches. Allow employees to have appropriate personal items and photographs on their desks.

- Living plants. Bring plants into your office space to help you relax and open up.

- Running water. Include a fountain in your office, as well as in your front lobby.

- Organic shapes. Include loose-flowing shapes in wall art or window coverings.

- Mirrored views. Hang a large mirror on your wall to bring available views of nature into your office.

- Relax the back. Purchase a desk chair that allows you to lean back with comfort security.

Use a mirror to bring views of nature into your office interior. Visually surrounding yourself with nature will remind you that "letting go" is part of the nature's cycle, and not something to be feared.

Living plants increase the amount of oxygen in a space during daylight hours. The extra oxygen will help you loosen up on a cellular level.

The creativity gua

Two vertical yang lines support a horizontal yin line, creating the condition for erupting fullness. This fullness is associated with the Creativity phase of the ba gua life cycle: fall, the harvest, and a time of joyful plenty. Located in the middle right-hand section of your office, the Creativity gua calls upon the creative forces that are born of observation and experience. The I Ching advises engaging this energy by becoming "totally open and unprejudiced toward the object of your inquiry. Go beyond objectivity into pure observation and acceptance." This acceptance requires that we let go of how we thought things were going to turn out and open to acceptance of what is. This acceptance brings its own wealth of creative inspiration. Although this gua is associated with Metal energy, it is not focused on the refinement aspect of Metal (the way the Helpful People gua is), rather it is focused on observation and neutral acceptance of those observations (the ancient Chinese formula of the scientific method).

Bringing rainbow colors into your Creativity gua can be as simple as purchasing a pad of brightly colored self-adhesive notes.

Consider opening to an experience of the world around you by placing any of the following objects in your Creativity gua.

- Binoculars or magnifying glass for observation

- Small terrarium or miniature ecosystem where you can watch natural cycles

- Gifts from the earth, such as ore, natural crystals, pinecones, copper,

- Symbols of the harvest, including autumnal colors and falling leaves

- Pictures of an open lake

- Rainbow colors or white (representing a balanced blend of all the colors)

- Open containers

- Toys, puzzles, and playful objects

- General nature scenes

- Pictures of children engaged in spontaneous play

- A photograph of yourself as a child

- An item symbolic of what you enjoy spending time and money on (hobbies, personal pleasures)

The Buddhist art of "neutral observation" can be energetically represented by a pair of binoculars or a chair beside a window with a view of passersby.

The rainbow colors captured in this wall mural are accentuated by the matching colors in the couch cushions, making this office a fun and playful place to be.

This interior designer balances the weight of running a successful and demanding business with the spontaneity and fun evident in his office.

Creative power of observation

The Chinese were avid nature observers, believing that the answers to the mysteries of life were to be found in the rhythms and patterns of the natural world. Observing nature and extracting predictable patterns from their observations were the foundation of their science. They would then apply these patterns to other life aspects, believing that what they found to be true in microcosm would also be true in macrocosm. Observation was, therefore, a highly valued art form. More than a way of knowing, it became a mode of tuning in to the vibrations and underlying causes behind the observations themselves.

In our modern business world, the same powers of observation can be used to understand and serve the needs of your business's target market. As shown in the Planning Cycle Chart, the six stages of the planning cycle are:

Planning cycle chart

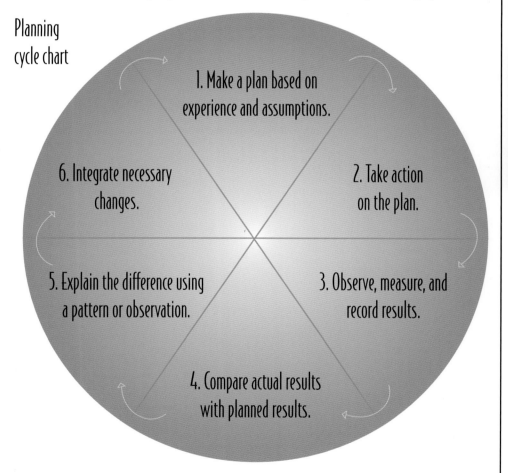

1. Make a plan based on experience and assumptions.

2. Take action on the plan.

3. Observe, measure, and record results.

4. Compare actual results with planned results.

5. Explain the difference using a pattern or observation.

6. Integrate necessary changes.

Hang a picture of nature in your office as a reminder that the answers to most business questions can be found by observing the rhythms and patterns of nature.

At every point in this process, modern businesses use the powers of observation and patterning to make sense of their world, forecast probable scenarios, and analyze results.

The following feng shui adjustments are designed to highlight humankind's interdependency on the natural world and support our intention to honor nature's sharing of her wisdom and insight with us.

- Incorporate water. As a primary force that brings life to all things, water is both powerful and wise. Your water can be a fountain, a small vase, a picture of a lake, or even a sound machine playing a recording of falling rain.

- Add a patio garden or terrarium. Gardens keep us in touch with nature's cycles and remind us of her wisdom. A small terrarium under a glass case can be included in almost any office plan, and an employee area with access to the outdoors makes a great place for a patio garden.

- Hang a wind chime. Symbolic of the wisdom that is borne upon the winds, wind chimes have been used for centuries to connect humans with the forces of nature.

- Display crystals or gemstones. The treasures of the earth manifest in many forms. Whether you choose to display crystals, gemstones, or iron ore in your office, use it as a reminder of the earth's fecundity.

- Include a rock or sand garden. Use this tool to loosen rigid thoughts and allow subconscious patterns to emerge.

A sound machine can bring the soft sound of running water into the office without the maintenance or mess of a fountain.

You will be surprised at the ability a small sand garden has to loosen rigid mental constructs and open you to new ways of thinking.

Heaven— the power of refinement

The Heaven trigram initiates a process of refinement and release. R. L. Wing's translation reflects, "Cast away from yourself all random interferences and unorganized trivia. . . . You should carefully conserve and direct your resources." Strict discrimination is recommended to make certain that you are not squandering your precious resources of money, time, and energy on clients, projects, or services that are not a good match for your personal energy. So how do you know if they are a good match? A good match energizes you, leaving you feeling more able to take on the next project. A poor match ends up taking more energy and resources than it provides, and leaves you feeling unappreciated, drained, or resentful.

Whether or not you enjoy decor as minimalist as this, aggressively remove any unnecessary items or decor objects from the Heaven trigram area of your office.

The helpful people gua

Located in the front right-hand corner of your office, the Helpful People gua is your place for letting go of everything that no longer serves you. Dedicated to refinement and release, the Metal-energy pattern of Helpful People makes it easier to let go. Use any of the following adjustments to help you to increase your powers of discernment and give you the added boost to release anything that no longer serves you and your business.

- Circular shapes. The circle is the most yang shape of all and will cast away from its center any "unrefined" or nonessential energies.

- Metal objects. Anything made of metal will sharpen your cutting edge. Use this to your advantage by bringing Metal items into the Helpful People area. Just as a sharp blade can make cutting tomatoes easier, a little Metal in Helpful People can support your efforts to get rid of what you do not want around.

- The color white. White helps you focus and increases clarity. If you need to get clear on something, add white.

- Organized and clutter-free. Make it a priority to keep this area of your office well organized and clutter-free. Nothing will muddle your thinking processes more than clutter.

- Trash can. If you have been wondering where in your office to put a large trash can or shredder, this is the place. You can make it decorative, bringing a little fun to the letting go process.

Add Metal to the Helpful People gua if you need help with letting go.

This decorative trash can is perfect in the Helpful People gua. Placing your trash can here can aid you in refining and letting go of those projects, clients, and commitments that no longer serve you.

Releasing "unrefined" clients

The I Ching teaches that some client energies are "pure," and some are "unrefined." A pure client is one whose energy is a good match for yours. This client seems to understand you, think like you, and value the same things you do. The unrefined client represents a mismatch, someone who is not good for your system. Just as some foods will nourish one body and poison another, the same clients who drain your business could nourish others. The Creative trigram suggests that it is imperative to your health and the success of your business that you release those clients who do not match your essence and send them to someone whose services would better match their needs and desires.

This teaching runs contrary to the Western notion that you must secure your market share by scrambling to "win over" every possible client, regardless of what it might cost you energetically. Focusing on dollars instead of energy expenditures, this notion can leave you feeling drained and joyless in your business. To apply the Creative energy in your business, mentally track the clients you have worked with in the past month. This is a quick painless process. You simply conjure up a mental image of that person and ask yourself if they have given you as much energy (in the form of money or other exchanges) as they took from you. If they required more effort, more time, or more scrambling, it is possible they took more energy from you than you expected and did not adequately compensate you. If they appear darkened or gray when you picture them, they are draining your energy. If they appear luminescent and bright, they are good clients for you.

A refusal to let go of projects, services, and clients that drain the business's resources has ruined more businesses than any other single factor. Whether it is the quick but mismatched expansion, or the enticing but demanding client, no business can sustain ventures that require more energy than they give back. Discern where in your business you might be ignoring this simple but powerful truth.

Free up your time and energy for those clients who are a good match for your business by pruning your desktop file. Removing the business cards of clients or businesses that drain you leaves you better able to attract your perfect clients.

This process of continual refinement holds incredible power, the power of clarity. As you receive clarity on who you are and which types of clients are a good match for your energy and gifts, your personal energy field increases in strength. By eliminating drains and focusing your efforts on clients who energize and excite you, your clarity increases and the chi of your business grows stronger. You begin to attract even more like-minded clients, initiating an ongoing cycle of support, rather than remaining stuck in an ongoing cycle of frustration and disappointment.

Disentangle yourself from questionable business relationships or practices by untangling your computer cords. Chaotic views, such as a jumble of computer cords, force you to disassociate from your physical environment. This disassociation results in general feelings of separation from others and from life.

If you know that you need to release unhealthy clients or projects, yet still find it difficult, use running water. A small fountain or a mister bottle next to your desk will generate the negative ions you need to physically release energy.

Releasing "unrefined" projects, products, and services

Just as the unrefined client can drain your business, so can unrefined services or projects. Let us say you are tempted to include a new product line or to bid on an enticing upcoming project. In the I Ching, the Creative trigram warns that not all products or projects will bring a positive return. "Know where your actions will lead. Know when not to act." This is the mark of the master. There are times when not bidding, not expanding, or not launching a new line will actually strengthen your existing business.

Go through your files, removing all files related to projects with which you no longer want to associate yourself. Physically removing them from your active files will help you eliminate the energy of these projects from your business. Place the projects in a temporary file in the Helpful People area of your office to aid you in bringing these projects to closure.

Caught up in the excitement of expanding her office to include a full-time training center, one professional organizer was trying to decide just how much space she needed. Up to this point, she had taught a weekly meditation class and was considering leasing more square footage than the new center alone would require so that she could continue to teach the class.

While considering the enterprise, she realized she would actually be paying over $600 monthly for the extra space, and that the class only brought in $650 a month. Asking herself what it was about teaching the class that she loved, she realized that she loved the scheduled opportunity to slow down and sit still for an hour.

With many other teaching opportunities available to her, it was not the teaching, but the sitting that she really needed. With this realization came the clarity that continuing to teach the meditation class would actually drain the time and money resources she needed to bring her primary dream, the new center, to life. She decided to let the class go and attend a weekly meditation group led by someone else.

Refining your files

Bring clarity to your business by sorting through and cleaning out your files. Simply scanning the titles of your files will alert you to how you have envisioned your business and where your focus lies. If you realize that the focus depicted in your files is not what you desire, use the Feng Shui Your Files Chart below to sort through and re-create your filing system.

Feng shui
your files chart

1. Mentally divide your files into two main sections: active and storage.

2. Physically separate your active and storage files.

3. Arrange your active files according to your business organization.

4. Create new labels for all of your folders.

5. Let go of past-time files.

6. Create files for your new work.

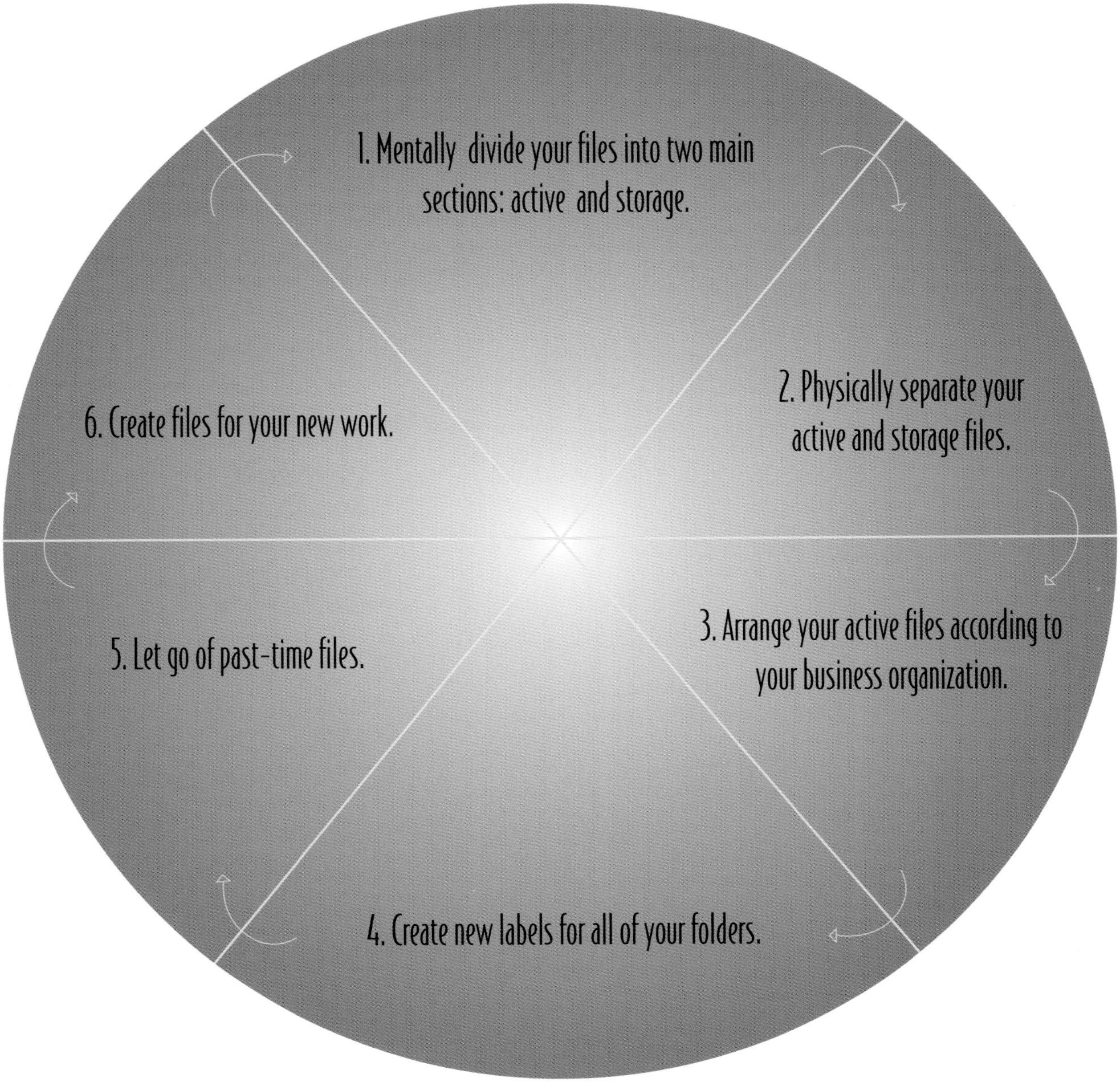

Setting up your files

Divide your files into two main sections: active and storage.

Your active files should include:

- clients with whom you are currently working,
- tax information for the current year,
- current vendors,
- current projects.

Your storage files should include:

- clients with whom you have not worked in the past year,
- tax information more than one year old,
- vendors you have not used in over 12 months,
- inactive projects.

Use different colored files for each section such as consulting work, presentations, and passive income, i.e. a book or product line.

Physically separate your active and storage files. Move your current files to the area most easily accessible, such as of your vertical-stacking file. Place your storage files in the filing area that is least convenient to access, such as the filing cabinet in the back room.

Arrange your active files according to your business organization. Your files are a visual representation of your business structure. By organizing your files, you bring clarity and control to your business. You might arrange your files into sections for each service that you offer, for each product line, or for each target market. Any additional business components, such as personal training and development would require yet another file section.

Create new labels for your folders. Giving your old and new folders the same look will integrate them visually and energetically. Creating new and different labels will help you better define the boundaries of your business because you will know exactly who you are serving and what you are doing.

Let go of past-time files. When relabeling, you will find that some files are "past time" for you and that you no longer need them. Discover the power and thrill of removing these files and tossing them into the dumpster.

Create files for your new work. Files serve as containers, holding the energy of a client, task, project, or product line. If you desire to attract new clients or projects into your business, create a new container to hold the energy you desire to attract. You will be amazed at how the new files you create fill up with new clients and projects.

Use three-inch file labels instead of the standard two-inch type so that your labels are easy to read. This makes it simple to find what you are looking for and reduces the feeling of frustration and confusion that settles over many of us simply upon opening the filing-cabinet drawer.

This filing cabinet is as beautiful as it is functional, enhancing the energy of all the client files stored within.

The personable office

Want your office to be an engaging, supportive, and uplifting place to be? An office has a strong "life force" when the chi energy of the human element and the chi energy of the space are in harmony. To bring your external environment into harmony with the natural patterns and rhythms of your body is a primary feng shui objective.

As helpful as wind chimes and crystals may be, the best way to create harmony is to infuse your environment with your personality. If the colors, fabrics, art objects, and pen holder tell the world more about who you are on the inside, your space will foster and support your personal growth.

Who says your home office has to be indoors? This client transformed a patch of dirt in the backyard into her personal haven. Her haven reflects her personality and provides a place for brainstorming sessions and self-reflection.

Make your office as distinctive as you are. This wall clock and bulletin board express the occupant's zany and eclectic style. Consider every item on your walls as an expression of your life force, and work to bring them into alignment with that force.

Creating a personable office requires that you become familiar with your favored modes of expression. Do you know which colors relax you? Energize you? Sedate you? How would you express yourself through fabrics, lighting, shapes, cultural artifacts, or design trends? This chapter takes you through an explorative journey into many different ways clients have created a personable office, custom-tailored to suit their personalities, styles, and ambitions. As you see what others have done, play with options that might work for you. Take one client's color choice and another's filing idea. Combine all your pieces together in an office environment that helps you live a fuller happier life.

Do not limit yourself to walls. Your window coverings also play a role in personalizing your office. Soft flowing drapes such as those shown below, bring water energy into the office, allowing for flow and movement.

Personal items

In Black Hat Tibetan Buddhist feng shui, Grand Master Lin Yun emphasizes the importance of a category he calls "Other." After going through all the traditional feng shui adjustments for elevating and improving the energetic vibration of a space, he takes special care to remind his listeners that the best feng shui adjustment objects are those that have personal significance and relevance for the individual. The American psychologist, Carl Jung, referred to the ability of certain objects to hold sway over the mind of an individual as "numinosity." Objects with numinosity, i.e. personal significance, are always going to have a stronger influence over your mental and emotional states than objects that are not personally significant.

Personal objects generate "numinosity," Jung's term for items of personal significance that activate a person's "chi."

With that in mind, work spaces that are decorated with objects that are meaningful to you will have a greater ability to support you, heal your heart, and inspire your soul to greatness than a bland corporate environment. This does not mean that each employee should be free to litter his or her desk with one hundred mementos, beanie babies, or family portraits. Taken too far, a "personalized desk" can become a distraction and a means of avoiding the work at hand. However, within reason, personal objects empower employees to perform more proficiently than they would otherwise.

Wall art

What you place on the walls of your office will provide the visual backdrop for every thought, conversation, and experience you have there. In fact, the walls are a part of your thoughts, your conversations, and your experiences. When selecting wall art, pay attention to how a particular piece makes you feel and what you think about when you look at it. Art that was created by an artist during a time of turmoil, personal grief, or mental instability is not recommended. Before you buy a piece of art for your walls, make certain that the experience of the artist was akin to how you experience your world. Otherwise, you may be inviting an energy into your space that may work against you.

It is not every day you see part of a Volkswagon® "bug" transformed into a piece of wall art. Expect the unexpected is the message here.

The blank concrete walls of this artist's studio are a deliberate backdrop to the vibrant paintings she creates on her easel.

This art director painted the word "art" on the Fame wall of her office in different languages. Everyone who enters her office is thereby encouraged to associate her with artistic creations.

Photography

A photograph is a snapshot of life. Frozen in time, photographs can help us use the energy of a particular moment or experience as an anchor. This anchor can remind us of our goals, values, and deep desires at times when we might otherwise forget. Even if the photograph is not of a personal experience, because photographs are born from someone's reality, they represent what is possible in the "real world." Use photographs that give you hope, open your heart, and raise your consciousness. If you feel loving, kind, in awe, inspired, motivated, understood, or peaceful when looking at a particular photograph, bring that experience into your office by hanging the photograph on your wall.

Photographs function as anchors, reminding us of our goals, values, and deep desires when we might otherwise forget.

Collages

A collage is a creative act that gathers the power of words, colors, images, fabrics, and small items together into a collective energy field. As a collective force, a collage works on the level of the subconscious, altering underlying beliefs and replacing self-defeating behaviors with more positive alternatives. Indeed, shamans and psychotherapists alike have used collages because of their ability to affect the psyche in such a primal and personal way.

Making your own collage. Anyone can explore and express their inner world with collage as their artistic medium. Collage allows you to take colors, phrases, and images created by someone else and combine them into your own masterpiece. Your collage will be an expression of how you see the world and your role within it. What you choose to use and how you arrange the pieces will give voice to hidden parts of you, bringing these parts to your awareness and allowing your hidden self a rare opportunity for expression and potential healing.

Once you have gathered your materials together, create the right mood for creative expression of your inner world. Poets and writers have often waited months for just the right mood to strike them before engaging in their creative acts. Spend some time establishing just the right mood for your collaging experience. Consider playing inspirational music, scenting the air with essential oils or incense, lighting candles, meditating, singing or chanting, or dancing before sitting down with your materials. Then, let your materials speak for you. There is no right or wrong in collaging, there is only expression. Ask only to be true to that which is within you, and you will find joy in your creation.

This unusual collage is a combination of decoupage and custom papers, some of which are arranged to look like tiles. The owner hangs inspirational items and quotes from the hooks, instead of coats.

The following list can help you generate ideas for things you would like to include in your collage.

- Images from magazine pictures that evoke a desired mental or emotional state

- Your own photographs of friends, associates, personal experiences and travels

- Items you found in nature, such as feathers, twigs, dried flower petals, pinecones, nuts, roots, or moss

- Craft materials that speak to you, such as beads, leather strips, cork, glass, tiles, crayons, oil pastels, or colored pencils

- Industrial materials, such as bolts, hinges, sheet metal, nails, or recycled objects, that you can relate to and tell a story with

- Fabric pieces and lace that communicate through texture, touch, and color

- Paint or color blocks made from any materials that have an emotional charge for you

- Pictures or cards that others have made for you, such as your child's artwork from school or a friend's thank-you note

- Kanji symbols that evoke an energy pattern that you want to include in your collage

- Words or affirmations that hold special meaning for you

Collages allow you to access intuitive knowledge through playful creative expression.

Paintings

There is very little hiding in the human heart that has not been expressed somewhere in a painting. Rich in meaning, paintings have long served as a favorite medium for expressing the self and its relationship to other energies. Whether you are drawn to watercolors, line drawings, woodcuts, or oil paintings, a well-selected piece of art can bring a tremendous life force into your work space.

Auspicious themes

Grounded in the natural world, ancient feng shui masters advised using artwork with certain themes in the workplace. These themes were thought to bring powerful archetypal energies to aid and assist the business.

Horses. During the T'ang Dynasty, horses were a popular gift, given as a tribute to China from many countries in central and western Asia. In fact, Emperor Ming Huang was said to have had over 40,000 riding mounts in his stables. Horses represent the power and strength to take advantage of the opportunities life gives you.

Musical instruments. Paintings of someone playing an instrument was considered auspicious because the Chinese found musical performances to be a vital means of understanding each other. By giving rapt attention to the person performing, one comes to know not only what moves the musician but what moves all human hearts. Whoever understood the roots of human motivation was assured of succeeding in business.

Cranes. The crane is a symbol for success with longevity. Although many business ventures can bring short-term profits, the crane represents the ability to realize long-lasting returns on an investment. Like cranes, pine trees are also a symbol of longevity and are known for being tenacious and enduring where other trees fail to grow.

Sailing ships. The full sails that carry the ships home represent a fullness of Wind energy. Wind is associated with wealth and opportunity and is the bringer of sudden and unforeseen riches (e.g. a "windfall" opportunity).

The blue heron is the symbol of self-realization and the power of inner knowing. If you place a picture of a blue heron in your space, you must be willing to see the truth of your motives, actions, feelings, dreams, inner strengths, and inner weaknesses.

Flowing water. Water is said to carry the influence and power of emperors to far away lands and to carry the wealth and richness of those lands back home. To sit beside flowing water is to benefit from all the world's achievements. If water flows directly toward you, however, you will be swept away by its power. Make certain you place a painting with flowing water at the side of you, rather than directly in front of you.

Green grass and healthy plant life. The kinship between humans and the natural world is recognized here. Situations in which the grass grows green and healthy will also be beneficial for humans. Places where plant life withers and dies will produce difficulties for humans as well.

People gathered together. Groupings of people indicate the power of kinship and the awareness that each person's activities should benefit the entire community. Even when one has to go away and follow a path that carries him far from his kin, he always returns to the fold of community to share the wisdom of his journey.

Mountains covered with trees. The penetrating power of wood on top of a mountain (stillness) is considered the perfect formula for enlightenment. The enlightened person makes decisions that elevate the entire social order, as well as acquiring great personal wealth and good fortune. The sun shining above a tree-covered mountainside is especially auspicious, as the sun is another enlightenment symbol.

Swimming goldfish or koi. Fish are at home in the element of water, which represents abundance. Often kept by royalty, the Chinese bred koi and goldfish. This ongoing breeding represents humans' attempts to partner with nature to create something unique and never before experienced.

Flowers. Each flower is richly symbolic, yet flowers in general represent the ability of the feminine—a soft, receptive, unfolding energy—to withstand the harshness of winter and be reborn again each spring. As the flower opens itself to receive sunlight and nourishing rain, so the feminine opens each of us to a greater understanding of ourselves and our common humanity. Flowers also represent the ability to enjoy and appreciate great beauty.

Dragons. The symbol of dynamism and change, dragons are mythic creatures said to breathe life force into all beings. There are many dragons in Chinese lore, each one representing something different. The general meaning of dragons, however, was that powerful and sudden change—growth, movement, excitement—was inevitable.

Themes to avoid

The following themes are thought to represent energies that would be somehow harmful to the business.

Waterfalls. Running water is a blessing, representing wealth and abundance, but a rushing waterfall is too much of a good thing. Related to chaos, death, and supernatural forces, waterfalls will bring more energy than is usually desired into an office.

A frozen lake or pond. When water freezes, it loses its ability to flow. For a business, flow represents cash flow and no business can survive for long without adequate cash flow.

Monkeys. Monkeys were seen as curious creatures whose penchant for pleasure got them into trouble. Often associated with excess, monkeys are considered symbolic of a company that spends too much too quickly.

A cliffside or ledge. Precarious positions are to be avoided in feng shui. The volatile energy of a cliff has the momentum to carry anyone nearby over its edge.

Decor choices

Lighting

When an issue or work project becomes confusing, shed light on it. Without adequate lighting, no one functions optimally. Ideally, you should have a combination of both natural and artificial (task) light available to you while you work. If you work graveyard shifts or are unable to have natural light, raise the level of illumination to counter the loss. Outdoor light usually ranges between 10,000 and 100,000 lux, while many lit interiors struggle by with 2,000 lux or less.

The lighting you select should also reflect and express your personality. Lighting fixtures have become the design statement of the twenty-first century. There is a huge range of fixtures available from "lighting artists" around the world. From the high-polished steel of Giancarlo Fassina to the washi-paper creations of Isamu Noguchi, your lighting choices communicate a wealth of knowledge about your preferences, style, and income level.

Fabrics and textures

Fabrics. Fabric is infinitely creative and activates both our visual and kinesthetic senses. No matter what your style, chances are you can find a piece of fabric to bring it out and give it expression. Once you find a piece of fabric you like, you can incorporate it into your work space in a number of creative ways.

Try covering your:
- desk chair,
- bulletin board,
- cubicle wall,
- windows,
- monitor,
- trash can,
- filing cabinet,
- keyboard.

You can also hang framed fabric on your wall like a picture or create a runner for your credenza.

If your cubicle is flooded with the fluorescent lighting of earlier years, remove the bulbs directly above your work area and light your space with lamps.

This wall divider is made from cotton muslin, delighting the senses and linking the office with the natural world.

Fabric is an easy way to customize your bulletin board. With just a few minutes and a few dollars, you can shift the energy of your office to more fully reflect your personality.

130

Textures. In addition to fabrics, you can bring a play of textures into your office to soothe or stimulate you. Consider the surface of your desk. Is it smooth like glass or rough like wooden planks? What about the seat of your chair? Does energy slide off it or get slowly absorbed? Texture allows you to balance the exchange of energy between yin and yang states of being. Rough, porous textures absorb the energy and slow the chi down, creating a more yin environment. Yin offices hold a more relaxing, nurturing, and slower energy than yang offices. Smooth, slick, or hard surfaces that reflect light and energy, rather than absorb, create more yang energy. Yang is the energizer, the motivator. It is what propels people to action, gets things moving, and keeps them going. To increase yang, incorporate more smooth reflective surfaces into your office design.

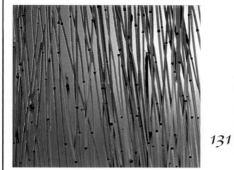

Thatch

131

Bear Grass

Brick, wood, metal, and laminates combine to make this a versatile and elementally balanced workspace.

Rose Petals

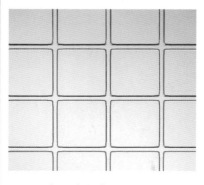

These organic materials are pressed between Plexiglas® creating a referent to the natural world that can replace a wall in your workspace.

Imprinted squares

Paint

Colors evoke different mental and emotional states. Although it is true that your personal experiences and memories can alter the effect that a particular color has on you, there are general physiological and psychological effects that can guide you in selecting the right paint color for your office.

The white palette. White does not need to be sterile. A favorite color choice for office buildings, white has some strong advantages. It is an intellectual color that sends blood to the brain, increasing mental activity. Unfortunately, this means that is drains the physical body and can make people feel tired faster. You can keep the benefits of mental clarity while eliminating the drawbacks of a pure white by tinting your white with a warm color, such as pink, gold, or peach. Just a slight hue can relieve the physical body of the constant strain of white. When mixing whites, be certain that your tones are all either warm or cool, or what you thought was a color scheme will turn out looking like a mistake. Also, when your white tones are too similar, one will look like a faded version of the other. You will need a strong enough contrast between tones that the color shift comes across as intentional.

Off-whites add a depth of combinations to the white palette. Mellow off-whites and creams add age and character to an office, taking the edge off and softening the overall effect. Avoid off-whites that look "dirty," however, as they might cause clients to regard the business as uncared for and poorly managed.

A white workspace helps to keep people focused and mentally alert. Too much white, however, often results in sarcastic workers. This business chose to add color to an all-white room through their quilt patches.

The neutral palette. Gray, taupe, stone, buff, silver sage, espresso brown, umber, and ocher make up the neutral palette. Selecting a neutral palette for an office aligns the work that happens there with the cycles and rhythms of the natural world. Neutral schemes have a grounded quality that is difficult to match in other color schemes. Rush mats, plaster walls, earthenware pots, and the coarse muslin of primitive cultures are subconsciously introduced through neutral colors. Neutral does not always have to mean primitive, however. Neutral colors can bring to mind the sophistication of Japanese rock gardens and the lure of Italian cafés. Unlike whites, the neutral palette supports the physical body, relaxing the muscles and soothing tension and strain. For offices where physical labor is a daily occurrence, consider a neutral palette. Avoid neutral palettes in businesses with a high-tech focus or a trendy clientele.

Neutralize a color scheme by "washing" the paint after application. A toning wash gives depth and age to the ordinary.

The bright palette. The bright palette energizes and excites both mind and body. Bold and artistic, bright colors are an excellent choice for businesses that need new energy and creative solutions to old problems. Red arouses the emotions and gets the blood flowing. Orange stimulates the social centers of the brain and yellow gets people talking. Try incorporating both cool and warm colors in a bright palette, such as lemon-yellow curtains against a Mediterranean-blue wall.

If you have a weak immune system, avoid bright bold colors. Your body will try to match the vibration of the color, which will drain you quickly and leave you feeling exhausted by three o'clock in the afternoon.

This formal office interior is enlivened through the vibrant oranges, reds, and greens of a painting. A painting with more-somber colors would leave this office feeling flat and lifeless.

Bright colors are not for everyone, but they are ideal for areas dedicated to brainstorming and thinking outside the box. When using bright red, avoid using white. If employees look at a white surface after looking at a red surface, they will see green (red's complement). This ocular effect can create nausea and other stomach problems.

The cool palette. The cool palette works best in office settings that focus on healing, rejuvenation, and release. Blue-greens aid in metabolic balancing and true blue soothes, reflects a freedom of spirit, and relaxes the body. The danger of choosing a cool palette is that productivity in the workplace tends to decline. To keep a cool palette more active, try a softer shade of turquoise or add a little yellow to your green. You can also accent with white, which will bring in contrast and quicken the pace.

A note on green. Green rests right in between the cool palette and the warm palette, carrying energy from one to the other, and balancing out catabolic and anabolic processes in the body. It is difficult to go wrong when adding green to an office environment, as it symbolizes the healing, balancing properties of nature and stimulates the body's own natural healing processes. Avoid strong green/red combinations in an office, however, as this combination results in higher sick leave among employees than other green combinations.

A soft sage green is both calming and rejuvenating. Use green to enliven a sterile environment or soothe a frenzied one.

The blues and greens of this painting work with the white walls to create a relaxed yet alert mental state in this art studio.

The warm palette. Sun-drenched coral, citrus yellow, and blossoming peach all warm and enliven a room. They are associated with emotions of joy, happiness, and radiant enthusiasm. Although it is great to have cheerful people around, the visually active nature of these colors bounces light around a room, stimulating the eye and keeping the energy moving. While eye-catching appeal is ideal for packaging and graphic design, too much of these colors in your office will make it difficult to concentrate on what is in front of you. To keep interactions upbeat without creating distractions, select softer muted tones. Try gold in place of chrome yellow, or a terra-cotta version of orange. Mixing warm tones with green also creates a stabilizing effect.

The coral, lime, and citrus colors in this collage seem to jump off a white wall, enlivening and rousing the entire room. After adding this collage, the business owner felt a renewed surge of creative energy.

The use of warm colors in advertising and print has been proven to catch the eye and draw the attention of viewers faster than cool colors. Use warm colors when you have only a few moments to attract your customers' attention.

Office stress relievers

Stress is a difficult part of the workday for many of us. How to handle and lower stress is a crucial part of a healthy office environment.

Music

Music is a powerful mood agent and can alter your state of consciousness. Although feng shui assigns sound energy in general to the realm of Wood, varying types of music create different effects in the body and mind. Whether you have a small radio, a set of headphones, or an entire surround-sound system, music can aid and support you. Experiment to see which types of music relax, rejuvenate, motivate, inspire, or calm you. Keep these CDs handy and pop them in whenever you are in need.

Water

Nothing relaxes like running water. Running water generates more negative ions than anything else besides lightening. The negative ions literally pull stress, which builds up like static-cling particles, off the body and induce a more tranquil state.

Fountains. The most commonly used feng shui adjustment for bringing water into your office is to add a small desktop fountain. Place your fountain within 18 inches of your computer monitor to use water to reduce electromagnetic vibrations, as well as adding the negative ions. If you have a fountain, make certain to keep it clean and running. Do not leave an empty fountain sitting on your desk, as fountains represent the flow of opportunities into your life.

Misting. Misting your office is another great way to generate negative ions and de-stress your office. Misting is especially helpful if you job-share with another person. At the start of your shift, clear their energy out of your space by lightly spraying your desk chair and the surrounding area. See Scent on page 138 for suggestions on which essential oils to add to your water.

Ringing a chime when you enter your office at the beginning of the day keeps the chi from stagnating and helps "awaken" the energy in your office.

Small desktop fountains can reduce electromagnetic radiation, as well as generate negative ions that can also reduce stress.

Fresh aromatic cedar needles make a better potpourri than artificially scented dried flowers. Cedar is a grounding scent that will make it easier for you to sit still longer.

Lavender eases both stress and worry, making it a helpful advocate in the office.

Scent

Essential oils can bring a field of French lavender, a California orange grove, or an English rose garden right of your work space. Our sense of smell provides immediate access to our emotions and moods. According to master herbalist John Steele, the olfactory epithelium (smell receptors at the back of each nostril) is the only part of the nervous system that is directly exposed to the atmosphere. Like music, scent can alter your mood, re-create memories, and clear your head. The effect of each scent is based on its vibration. True essential oils, made from the living cells of plants, vibrate at a frequency compatible with human beings. The vibration of artificial scents is not as compatible with living cells and can result in headaches, allergic reactions, and mental confusion.

Creating a balanced blend. Like perfumes, essential oils are characterized by "notes." A "top note" has a light fresh quality which is immediately present, due to the rapid evaporation rate of these oils. A "middle note" is the heart of the fragrance (which usually forms the bulk of the blend), with a scent that emerges slowly. A "base note" is a rich heavy scent that emerges last and lingers, acting as a fixative to stop the lighter oils from dispersing too quickly. A balancing blend will contain at least one oil of each note quality.

The following list will give you a rudimentary idea of which common oils fall into which categories:

- Top notes: Tea tree, bergamot, rosemary, eucalyptus, tangerine, lemon, and basil

- Middle notes: Geranium, chamomile, lavender, marjoram, rosewood, and rosemary

- Base notes: Sandalwood, patchouli, rose, jasmine, benzoin, frankincense, myrrh, spikenard

The Essential-oil Properties for Use in Feng Shui on pages 140–142 will give you an idea of how common oils have been used in the past. The best way to discover the energetic impact of an oil, however, is to test it on your own sense of smell. Place a drop on a tissue and inhale. Do not place essential oils directly on the skin. Tune in to the subtle body of the scent and note the shifts that occur once you encounter the oil's vibration. Some oils will give you an instant headache, others will cause you to breathe deeply and relax. You cannot know how an oil will affect you personally until you interact with it.

Combinations for relieving stress:

- Tea tree, geranium, and sandalwood

- Tangerine or mandarin, green tea, and ginger

- Juniper, orange, and rosewood

- Cedar, chamomile, and bergamot

Essential oils are made from herbs, flowers, roots, barks, fruits, leaves, and resins.

If you need more grounding, use base-note scents. For a lighter heart and cheerful spirit, use top notes.

Essential-oil properties for use in feng shui

Benzoin

An oil commonly used in incense, benzoin was said to drive away evil spirits. Feng shui applications include using benzoin to clear a room after an argument.

Bergamot

A sweet fruity scent. In an oil diffuser, its refreshing uplifting quality has made it a favorite for combating anxiety and depression.

Chamomile

Considered one of the nine healing plants by the Saxons and revered by the Egyptians, chamomile is used worldwide for its relaxing, de-stressing properties. Especially helpful in calming an upset stomach, nervous tension, or ulcers, chamomile blends can ease tensions and help to keep people from getting upset.

Eucalyptus

There are two primary types of eucalyptus, a broad-leafed peppermint variety and a lemon-scented variety. Aborigines use the peppermint variety to relieve fevers, whereas the lemon-scented variety is used to repel cockroaches. Medically, eucalyptus is often used to clear the sinuses and to ease muscular aches. Eucalyptus in the office encourages deep breathing, which oxygenates the body and clears the head.

Frankinscense

A deep base note, frankincense is grounding and comforting. Introduce frankincense into the office when you are feeling scattered and lacking focus. Frankincense is collected from small trees as a resin and is commonly used by both the Chinese and the Catholic church in incense.

Geranium

A strong rose-like scent, use geranium sparingly. Although used historically to reduce inflammation, including inflamed tempers, geranium can overpower the room and cause headaches.

Jasmin

A heady floral scent, the Chinese traditionally used jasmine to induce an overall feeling of optimism and confidence. A general feeling of euphoria and well-being makes this a favorite scent in office spaces, especially for salespeople.

Lavender

One of the most commonly used oils, lavender is like an herbal first-aid box. It is useful in combating daily upsets, as well as soothing emotions after a major trauma or shocking experience. For people who tend to worry a lot, lavender calms the mind and assists in the release of obsessive thoughts.

Lemon

A fresh citrus scent without the sweetness of other citrus fruits, lemon adds a clean refined sharpness to the atmosphere. When things feel confusing, use lemon oil to find clarity.

Marjoram

A warm woodsy and spicy scent, marjoram is considered fortifying as well as calming. Marjoram helps ground the energy in a room.

Myrrh

The use of myrrh has been common for over 3,700 years in both Eastern and Western medicine. Myrrh has a warming, drying property which made it important for embalming purposes. The Chinese use myrrh in feng shui to solidify a shifting energy. Because it is not liquid at room temperature, myrrh is more easily introduced into a room through incense.

Patchouli

A deep, earthy scent, patchouli is calming and grounding. Because the scent is heavy, it helps hold lighter scents in place when used in blends.

Rose

A deep sweet floral scent, rose will overpower just about any other scent if not blended correctly. The symbolism of roses is probably more intricate than that of any other flower, and its association with Venus, the goddess of love, has not gone unnoticed by perfume makers (rose oil from one of the 10,000 rose varieties is used in over 46 percent of men's fragrances and over 90 percent of women's). For feng shui purposes, it activates the senses and arouses the passions, making it a scent to avoid in office spaces.

Rosemary

A stimulant for the circulatory system, rosemary is often used to combat mental fatigue and nervous exhaustion. Rosemary has a fresh pungent herbaceous scent.

Rosewood

The production of rosewood oil is damaging to the South American rain forests, so the oil is being replaced by the synthetic form. As such, it has primarily perfumery use. Rosewood is said to aid headaches and lessen nausea.

Sandlewood

The sandalwood from East India is known for combating depression and uplifting the spirits. A deep, soft woodsy scent, sandalwood relaxes the muscles and has a general aphrodisiacal influence.

Sweet basil

A powerful aromatic scent, basil is known as a "cooling" herb, soothing nervous tension and general irritability. If anyone in your office is feeling grouchy, try adding basil.

Tangerine

More pungent and less intensely sweet than its cousin-scent mandarin, tangerine is refreshing and can rejuvenate the spirits and lagging energy in the late afternoon.

Tea tree

A deep, earthy scent, patchouli is calming and grounding. Because the scent is heavy, it helps hold lighter scents in place when used in blends.

Ylang Ylang

Said to have high, middle, and base note qualities contained within a single oil, Ylang Ylang is an aphrodisiac and is not usually appropriate for work settings.

Once you have selected oils beneficial to you, you need to bring those scents into the office. If you work in a space with other people, be careful how you scent the space. The three ways that work best in an office are:

Misters. In a four-ounce atomizer, combine 3 ounces distilled water with an ounce of essential oil. Shake, then mist your seat and the area surrounding your computer.

Lightbulbs. Before turning on your desk lamp, place a few drops of essential oil on the lightbulb. After you turn the lamp on, the heat from the bulb will evaporate the oil into the air, which you breathe.

Oil diffusers. Oil diffusers work by heating an essential oil to the evaporation point. Airborne molecules are transmitted to the body through the lungs.

Self-massage

While seated at your desk, listening in on a conference call, or even waiting for a web site to load, you can relax and reduce stress by performing a simple self-massage.

Shiatsu finger massage. The fingers are an easy place to access and manipulate your body's energy meridians. Each fingertip is either the starting point or ending point of a major energy meridian. By applying pressure to your fingers, moving slowly from the base of the finger out toward the tip, you can jump-start the flow of chi to all. The following diagrams will guide you through a simple finger massage designed to activate the flow of chi in the associated meridians.

The Finger Meridians below show a hand with points to each meridian. Pinky finger, lower-left side of nail is the small intestine, lower-right side of nail is the heart. Ring finger, lower-left side of nail is the triple heater. Middle finger, lower-right side of nail is the Pericardium. Index finger, lower-right side of nail is the large intestine. Thumb, lower-front of nail is the lung.

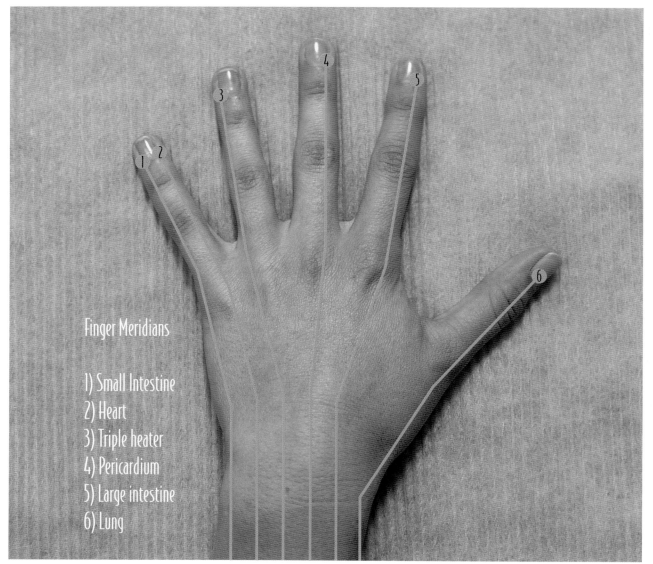

Finger Meridians

1) Small Intestine
2) Heart
3) Triple heater
4) Pericardium
5) Large intestine
6) Lung

44

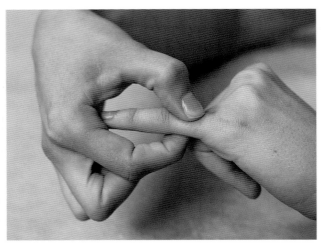

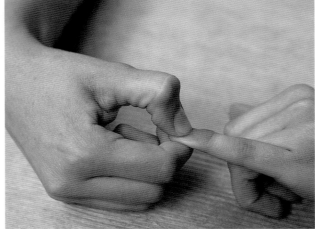

1 With your left palm facing downward, grasp the base of your left little finger between the thumb and the index finger of your right hand. Squeeze the little finger from the base upward to the tip, while creating an opposing force by lightly pulling away with your left hand.

2 Perform this for each digit on your left hand, moving from the little finger to the thumb. Then switch and do the same for the other hand, moving again from little finger to thumb.

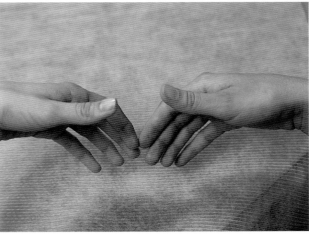

3 When you have massaged each of your fingers, interlock them and press palms outward, stretching the tendons on the inside of the arm. *Note: This exercise alone will greatly reduce the risk of carpal tunnel syndrome.*

4 Shake both wrists freely, with your fingers loose, feeling the tingling sensation in your hands.

Improving your social position

We all desire to feel valuable and important. Since the time and energy we give to work is such a large part of our lives, how we feel at work influences everything else. When you are the bottom rung of the corporate ladder, it is difficult to perform acts of greatness and inspiration.

Without waiting for a promotion or hard-walled office to elevate your status, you can shift your position in the corporate strata with a little feng shui ingenuity.

The office setup above uses low stacking files to separate two workspaces. This separation is not as effective as the vertical filing cabinet on the right.

This tall stacking filing cabinet does a better job of providing separation between workspaces, making it so that two people working side by side do not visually interupt each other.

Set yourself apart

Hard-walled executive offices provide privacy and physical separation from the masses. You can generate these same effects by creating boundaries in other ways.

Create your own divider. If you cannot have a hard-walled office, consider adding a ficus tree between you and the nearest coworker. This gentle, breathable separation will help keep harmony between you and your neighbor while strengthening your "relative position" in the work force. If you are stuck in a standard cubicle, see if you can get your boss to purchase a sliding cubicle door panel (shown below). Although it is not sound proof, this fabric panel provides control over your environment, which is often associated with a higher level of authority and responsibility. Other dividers, such as rolling fabric panels or sliding pocket doors, can turn just about any problem area into a workable space.

In tight spaces where you need all the elbow room you can get, consider a sliding pocket door between offices. The installation expense is comparable to a normal door.

Fabric panels on rollers are an artistic and simple way to set yourself apart. You can roll your panel into place when you desire additional privacy and roll it away again for more interaction.

This cubicle occupant installed a sliding fabric door panel so that he can actually close off his cubicle when not wanting to be disturbed.

Buffer with cork. Those coveted hard-walled offices are soundproof. Soundproofed privacy is an important rank signifier. You can create more privacy in your cubicle by going down to the local hardware store or home-improvement store and buying cork panels. Pin the cork panels up on the cubicle wall that separates you from your nearest neighbor. With cork as your sound-proofing agent, your phone calls will be a more private matter.

Use color. You will be surprised what happens when coworkers must cross over the threshold of your new brightly colored floor mat to enter your space. Their sense of arrival is heightened, which helps set your space apart from others.

Hang a sign. If you are in a cubicle and find that others are constantly invading your privacy, consider hanging a sign across your cubicle entrance that politely asks others to wait until you are ready for them. Such a sign might say, "Please come see me between 2 AM and 4 PM," or "Urgent Interruptions Only." My favorite is, "Only interrupt in cases of earthquake or chocolate." People appreciate your sense of humor and they stop interrupting so much.

Cork does not need to be boring to be effective. This cork bulletin board spans the length of the entire room and provides a needed sound barrier for private conversations.

By replacing gray cubical walls with colorful custom fabrics, this India office helps its employees assert their individuality and creativity, while maintaining an open team-friendly environment.

48

Make your office your own by covering your chair with a custom fabric. This is an excellent way to lay claim to a new position within a company.

Improve your seat

Nothing says hierarchy like the seating system. Does your boss rest comfortably in a $1000 chair while your back aches in a $40 chair? Interior design and business hierarchies are so intertwined that the names of certain office chairs are associated with various levels of command. The "Worker's" chair is the bottom level. This chair is functional, but typically has no armrests (why would a worker need to rest his arms?) and low or no back support. As a result, the worker has the least supportive, least comfortable chair of all. The "Secretary's" chair comes next. This chair is typically small, with a low back and small armrests. Next comes the "Executive" chair. Well-padded, with upholstery, high back, headrest, controllable tilt, and massive armrests, this chair is a command station. It represents the power and authority to give orders and have those orders carried out by someone else. Whether they are a worker, secretary, or executive, every employee knows exactly how valuable they are in the system by the chair they sit in.

When upholstering your chair, select your fabric carefully. Busy patterns will keep your mind moving, but make it harder to concentrate for any length of time; and darker colors are more grounding than light ones.

Buy a larger desk. If your desk size is under your control, buy yourself a larger desk. This investment will more than pay for itself come evaluation time. Just make certain that your desk is not larger than your boss's desk. This sends a message that you are a threat, rather than a help.

Add an L. Some desks can be improved by bringing in another piece of matching furniture to create an L-shaped desk from what was previously a rectangle. You can create an L-shaped desk by purchasing a simple trolley or cart, a filing cabinet the same height as your desk, or a small side table.

Clear off your desk. Your desk will look larger if it is cleared off. Those stacks and piles do not say, "I am important," they say, "I am overwhelmed." You might need to store some items in another area or even another room in order to get your desktop back under control.

This desk has wings that expand when needed for additional working space.

If you start your day in the middle of yesterday's mess, you will feel tired before you even begin. Take just two minutes at the end of each day to straighten your piles and ready yourself for the coming day.

A sign at your child's eye level and a colorful ribbon on the door can be gentle reminders that mom or dad is "at work."

Sometimes the easiest way to work with your children is to provide a place for them to create with you. If they are in the same room, they might just stay out of your hair.

The home office

Whether you are telecommuting or running your own home business, working from home is not a simple task. When you work from home, interruptions increase, boundaries dissolve, and the isolation demons come knocking. Take comfort. Knowing what some of these differences are can help you choose consciously how you want to interact with them.

Setting up boundaries

Everyone loves the freedom that comes with working at home, but increased freedom demands that you set your own boundaries or things can get out of balance fast. If you find yourself doing laundry when you should be writing a report, you need to put some boundaries in place.

Shut your door. If you have a physical door that shuts, shut it. Train family members to knock before entering and regard the shut door as a clear signal that you are not available. If your children walk right through the door, place a brightly colored sign at their eye level with their name on it, reminding them to knock before they enter.

Use ritual. If you do not have a physical door, you need to shut your mental door. Ritual is the key. Shutting a door is a ritual that separates the energy of one space from another. You must think of a ritual that you can maintain to separate your work energy from that of the living room or kitchen. Your ritual can include lighting a candle, turning on the CD player, or misting with water. What is important is that it shift the vibration in the space and in your body, to get both ready for the work mode.

This creative client transformed an unused closet into a miniature office that can be visually closed off from the rest of the family room simply by shutting the closet doors.

Screen your view. If you sit looking at the refrigerator, it will be difficult not to think about what to have for dinner. There are many ways to screen your view, depending on which room of house you are in. Plants, standing room dividers, and roll shades are all simple and inexpensive remedies.

Set up and keep office hours. Decide when you work best (e.g. 5:00 AM–1:00 PM) and designate those hours as office hours. Post a sign outside your office reminding family members of these hours. Put your office hours on your business phone message, letting clients and family alike know when you are available for business calls, to help everyone respect this boundary.

Use a separate phone line for business. Answer the business phone during your office hours only. Separate phone lines with different rings will help you not feel obligated to answer your business phone after hours. A separate phone line will also allow you to leave a business phone message that communicates professionalism, rather than that cute recording of your five-year-old. If you cannot afford a completely separate business line, get what is called a "distinctive ring" on your phone for a business number. That way when clients call, the phone has a different ring and you know whether or not to let your children answer it.

Before feng shui, this corner functioned merely as a display surface, while the client's desk was crammed into her bedroom.

After feng shui, the client transformed the unused corner into a functioning office space and was then able to restore her bedroom to a restful haven.

Sharing your space

When you work from home, you might find yourself sharing your work space with another person or another room function. Indeed, your "home office" might be a corner of the kitchen or the family room. You might share your computer with your children, or your spouse might run a business out of the same room. When you must share, there are ways to make this situation more conducive to your success.

Sharing your computer. School is out and suddenly your computer becomes the family hot spot, the center for gaming and internet surfing. Evening work can be difficult, too, if your spouse is home and wants his/her time on the "family" computer. You were taught it is nice to share, but if you do not stake and maintain your claim to your workspace, everyone in the family will suffer.

When this bedroom was converted into an office for two, it was challenging to arrange the desks in a way that supported both partners. The final placement allows each partner a primary view out the window and a sideways view of the other. Each one also has a solid wall behind them and a sideways view of the door. Avoid placements where partners are either facing each other or sitting back to back.

Sharing your office with your spouse. When there are two of you working from home, feng shui priorities shift. When setting up an office space for two, keep the following in mind.

- Create a sideways view of your office mate. Although it is important to have a view of the door, it is equally important to NOT have a direct view of your office mate. If you position your desks so that you are looking across your desk at the other person, you will have difficulty separating your energy and work tasks from that person. You will naturally get pulled into his/her phone conversations, paper shuffling, and sighs. Likewise, if you set up your desks with your backs to each other, you will feel vulnerable, exposed, and under attack by the other person. Go for the sideways view.

- Use headphones. Rarely are two people inspired and motivated by the same music at the same time. If you work better to music, use headphones so that your office mate is not affected by your choice.

- Muffle phone conversations. One of the most difficult things about sharing an office is the constant disruption caused by the other person's phone. If at all possible, stand up and leave the room to carry on phone conversations. If you cannot leave the room, swivel your chair so that you are not facing your office mate. Talking toward a wall will muffle the sound considerably and not break your spouse's concentration.

- Neutralize the center. Hang a 40mm–50mm crystal in the center of a shared work space to neutralize (disperse) your energies. Self-employed entrepreneurs are usually strong-willed people and move a lot of energy without knowing it. Hanging a crystal will help both of you be successful without interfering in the other's space.

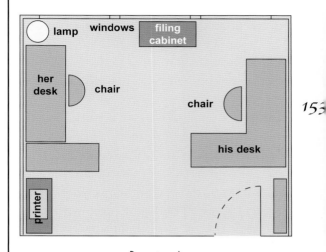

Drawing A

Before feng shui: Both the husband and wife sat with their backs to each other, facing a wall. Both of them felt vulnerable.

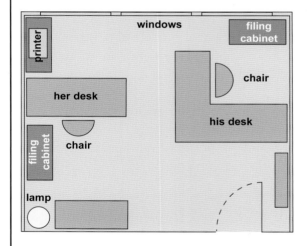

Drawing B

After feng shui: Each person has a view of a neighboring park out the window and a sideways view of the other person. Each has a sideways view of the door as well.

Coming to terms with paper

Most people who work from home love what they do and resist attending to the seemingly unimportant task of handling paper. The bummer is, paper is a crucial part of any home business and, the sooner you get it under control, the more effective and productive you will be.

Schedule a paper day once a week. Maybe Monday is your day to deal with paper; maybe it is Friday. Whatever day you decide, schedule a minimum of one hour that day to deal with your in-box, file your week's work away, and prepare any invoices or other documents for the coming week. If you already have a time during the week that you meet with a bookkeeper, this is the perfect time to deal with your paperwork.

Contain your paper. Every wonder why in-boxes got so popular? Paper needs to be contained. Usually clients tell me they keep papers on their desk because they are visual and tend to forget things if it is not directly in front of them. If so, take the papers scattered across your desk and place them in a wall-hanging unit that allows you visual access to the top of each pile. That way you can see what needs your attention and still keep your workspace free of clutter.

Get a system that works with the type of business you have. If you have tried organizing systems before and they did not work for you, it is not that your business could not benefit from organization, it is more likely that you need a different way of doing it.

Create an organizing system that works by:

- Identifying your visual needs. Do you need to see every scrap of paper all the time? How enclosed can your paper be and still be mentally available to you?

- Taking inventory of what you need to store. If you have to keep daily printed reports, you will need a different system than someone who only keeps a few invoices.

- Using containers and storage items that match your personality. If army green hanging files do not excite you, you will not want to spend your time or energy filing them. Try bright purple or spring green files instead.

This woven box is ideal for containing your paper. It fits both letter and legal size sheets, and can transform a messy dining-room table into a tidy pile within seconds.

Making money from home

If you have just recently started working for yourself, you are probably in shock. Not only are the paid vacations, health insurance, and sick days gone, but you also must to buy your own printer cartridges, do your own invoicing, and be your own secretary. Your home business needs to bring in enough money to pay for a bookkeeper, vacations, health insurance, and updated office equipment, as well as pay your salary. If it is currently not as lucrative as you would like, be certain to check the following factors.

Are you facing a wall? Nothing blocks your ability to generate business more than facing a wall. Successful business people must move energy. If your personal energy hits a wall every time you sit down at your desk, you will begin to anticipate defeat and move your own energy at a much slower rate. If your desk is a built-in and you cannot move it, place a picture of an expansive scene on the wall in front of you to give your energy somewhere to go.

Do you have living plants in the room? Living plants are a strong symbol of a growing thriving business. If you have a plant that is doing especially well, place one of your business cards underneath the plant, symbolically growing your business. Living plants also generate negative ions, which reduce stress, and mitigate the high electromagnetic fields that radiate out from your computer or cell phone.

Do you have heavy boxes on the floor? Heavy boxes will slow your business down. Remove them from the work area.

If you are feeling blocked, it is better to turn your desk to open up your view than to sit facing your door. If you opt for the view, be certain to place a small convex mirror somewhere on the desk so that you can still see your door, even though you are not facing it.

Working from home offers the advantage of a flexible schedule and low overhead, but requires that you set firm boundaries, both in time and space. Resist the temptation to let work cross over into personal time.

Where to place your office

If you have a choice as to which room in the home becomes the office, ask yourself which of the following considerations is most important to your well-being and make your choices accordingly.

Physically separate your work space as much as possible. If you find that you tend to get pulled into your normal home life, whether through children, chores, or other distractions, place your office as far away from the main flow of the living areas as possible.

Avoid the bedroom. Placing your office in your bedroom is a surefire way to generate resentment in your intimate partner. Better to take over the dining room or a corner of the living room than to let work invade the couple's domain. Also, if you have no intimate partner, allowing work to creep in and take over that space creates a "relationship replacement." Although this might feel comforting for awhile, because the energy of work is replacing the energy of lack, it blocks a new person from entering your life.

If you have to place your office in your kitchen, be certain to position it so that you do not look into the kitchen area. Place a rug as a visual divider on the floor to help separate these two spaces.

Use the ba gua map

Where your office is located in terms of the ba gua map influences the energy of the office.

Journey. This is a favorable sector for an office if you are starting a new business or a new undertaking.

Self-knowledge. Working in this sector is likely to focus on helping you discover more about who you are in the world than about making money.

Family and Ancestors. If you work a family business, this is the best possible place for you, unless you do not like how the business has run in the past. When that is the case, moving the office to the Journey gua helps initiate a new way of doing things.

Abundance. If you need more opportunities and financial stability, the Abundance gua is the best place for your office. This is especially important if your work is the sole income-producing job for the family.

Fame. If the well-being of your business requires selling yourself or your service, this is a great area for you. The expansive energy of the Fame area will help you interact with others, even if it is over the internet.

Intimate Relations. Not usually ideal for a home business, placing your office here can generate feelings of resentment in your spouse and turn your energy toward being a peacemaker for all kinds of work issues.

Creativity. If you are working for fun more than anything else, stay in Creativity. This gua is about being playful, opening to fullness, and finding joy in your work.

Helpful People. This area is the best for nonprofit organizations and other businesses that are community-oriented. This area can also bring supportive helpful energies in your business. One caution, placing your office in Helpful People could initiate more traveling. You will need to decide how much you want to be on the road.

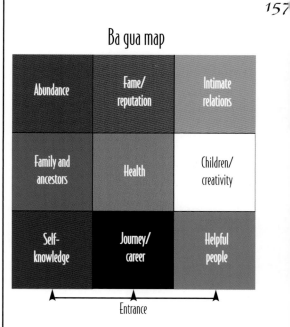

Ba gua map

Use this ba gua map and the information on the left to help you determine the best possible placement for your home office.

Acknowledgments

Many businesses and artists have contributed to the realization of this book. I am deeply grateful to Marla Dee, of Clear & Simple, for her paper-organizing strategies and clever containers. Many of the fine artists at Artworks Gallery in Park City, Utah, contributed original pieces of art, providing creative and unique feng shui office solutions. Susan Seymour's paper murals and Morag Totten's glass quilts are of special note. Susan Steele and Alan Bell of Henricksen Butler Design Group and Jill Jones of AJC Architects were particularly helpful in providing solutions for corporate settings, and the office solutions provided by Herman Miller are evidenced throughout the book. My thanks as well to 3-Form for their contemporary and organic wall solutions, and to Spacesavers for their novel paper-storage solutions. My professional associate, Roger Clark of Practical Fung Shui in Falls Church, Virginia, kindly provided photos of his proficient outdoor office solutions. Thanks, also, to Cynthia Herning and Wilmarie Huelskamp for opening their homes for photos.

In addition to interior designers, insightful graphic designers are also elemental for the feng shui'd office. My thanks to Janice Campbell, of The Very Idea, and Kris Sovereen, of Sovereen Design, for their work with corporate logos and identity packages. Much of the research and statistics, used to ascertain the effectiveness of the feng shui adjustments recommended in this book, were provided by Self Start, a consulting and training organization for beginning businesses.

The creative energy of Chapelle, Ltd. is evidenced, not only in the work of editor/designer Lana Hall, but in many of the interior photos. Chapelle's owner, Jo Packham, has spent years designing beautiful and creative workspaces for her team of talented artists, and many of those spaces are included in this book. My thanks to Kim Taylor, who was the first assertive employee to ask for her office space to be "feng shui'd."

Herman Miller (India)

AJC Architects

Henricksen Butler Design Group

Resources

SELF START, Inc., 703 E. 1700 S., Salt Lake City, UT 84105. Provides advanced business training and mentoring for feng shui consultants, professional organizers, and life coaches. Contact Sharon through her web site at www.selfstart.net, call 801-519-9161, or e-mail her at fstc@xmission.com.

The Feng Shui Training Center. Provides core training for feng shui practitioners. Contact them at www.thefengshuitrainingcenter.com, call 801-519-9161, or e-mail Sharon at fstc@xmission.com.

Clear & Simple. Provides the only professional organizer certification training program in the United States. They also provide organizing support for homes and businesses throughout the US. Reach them at ClearSimple.com or call 801-463-9090.

Photo Credits

3-form, Salt Lake City, UT: 131(r1)(r2)(r3)(r4), 133(t), 134(tr), 136(tr)

AJC Architects, Salt Lake City, UT: 2, 4(tl)(bl), 28(t)(b), 33(l)(r), 40(b), 42, 68(bl), 78(l), 89, 92–93, 95(t)(b), 115, 118(r), 122(t), 146(tr), 147(t), 158(c)

Artville (©1999)

Artworks Gallery, Park City, UT: 43, 83(l), 88(t), 90(l), 121(t), 125

DigitalVision Ltd., New York, NY/London, UK (©2001)

Getty Images, (©2000): PhotoDisc (©1993, 1995–96, 1999, 2000)

Herman Miller, Inc., Zeeland, MI: 3, 8, 9, 13, 17, 21(tl)(tr)(bl)(br), 29, 31(t), 47, 49, 54, 55, 114(t), 130(t)(c), 131(l), 134(b), 135(tr), 146(br), 147(b), 149(r), 158(t)

Henricksen Butler Design Group, Salt Lake City, UT: 6–7, 15, 22(r), 31(b), 39, 108, 118(l), 145(l)(r), 146(l), 158(b)

PhotoDisc (©1993, 1995–96, 1999, 2000)

Practical Feng Shui, Roger Clark, Falls Church, VA: 119(t)(b)

Scot Zimmerman, Salt Lake City, UT: 14, 24(b), 44(t)(b), 64(l)(r), 91, 132, 133(b)

Souvereen Design, Salt Lake City, UT: graphic designs 100, 136(l)(r)

Spacesavers, Winston-Salem, NC: 50

Very Idea, The, Salt Lake City, UT: graphic designs 97(bc)(tr)(br)

159

About the author

Sharon's background in psychology led her to develop an approach to feng shui that reveals how one's deep psychological patterns surface in one's external environment. Having worked with hospitals and healers of numerous disciplines, Sharon integrates Chinese medicine, traditional feng shui teachings, Jungian psychology, and shadow-therapy work into her feng shui consultations.

She delights in helping clients discover their purpose and align their lives to support that purpose. Sharon currently runs Self Start, a training center in Salt Lake City, Utah, that provides advanced business training and mentoring for feng shui consultants, professional organizers, and life coaches. Sharon balances her work life with two amazing boys and a joyful marriage.

Index

160